Perl 6 Essentials

Other Perl Resources from O'Reilly

Related titles

Programming Perl
Learning Perl
Perl Cookbook
CGI Programming with Perl
Computer Science & Perl Programming
Learning Perl Objects, References, and Modules
Games, Diversions & Perl Culture

Web, Graphics & Perl/Tk
Mastering Regular Expressions
Perl for System Administration
Programming Web Services with Perl
Perl Pocket Reference
Perl in a Nutshell
Perl Graphics Programming

Perl Books Resource Center

perl.oreilly.com is a complete catalog of O'Reilly's books on Perl and related technologies, including sample chapters and code examples.

Perl.com is the central web site for the Perl community. It is the perfect starting place for finding out everything there is to know about Perl.

Conferences

O'Reilly & Associates brings diverse innovators together to nurture the ideas that spark revolutionary industries. We specialize in documenting the latest tools and systems, translating the innovator's knowledge into useful skills for those in the trenches. Visit *conferences.oreilly.com* for our upcoming events.

Safari Bookshelf (*safari.oreilly.com*) is the premier online reference library for programmers and IT professionals. Conduct searches across more than 1,000 books. Subscribers can zero in on answers to time-critical questions in a matter of seconds. Read the books on your Bookshelf from cover to cover or simply flip to the page you need. Try it today with a free trial.

Perl 6 Essentials

Allison Randal, Dan Sugalski,
and Leopold Tötsch

O'REILLY®

Beijing · Cambridge · Farnham · Köln · Paris · Sebastopol · Taipei · Tokyo

Perl 6 Essentials
by Allison Randal, Dan Sugalski, and Leopold Tötsch

Published by O'Reilly & Associates, Inc., 1005 Gravenstein Highway North, Sebastopol, CA 95472.

O'Reilly & Associates books may be purchased for educational, business, or sales promotional use. Online editions are also available for most titles (*safari.oreilly.com*). For more information, contact our corporate/institutional sales department: (800) 998-9938 or *corporate@oreilly.com*.

Editor:	Linda Mui
Production Editor:	Emily Quill
Cover Designer:	Ellie Volckhausen
Interior Designer:	David Futato

Printing History:

June 2003:	First Edition.

ISBN: 0-596-00499-0
[M]

Table of Contents

Preface

There is nothing as scary to the average programmer (to the average human, really) as the single word "change." Change means taking the time to learn a new way of doing things. Changes can be annoying: moving to a new home, finding the shelves reorganized at your neighborhood computer store, or ordering your favorite beer at your favorite pub only to be told they don't make it anymore. But changes can also be good: a vacation on the beach, a promotion, a raise, finding the perfect shortcut to work that shaves 20 minutes off your commute. This book is all about change...the good kind.

Perl 6 isn't far enough along to support a book on the level of *Programming Perl*. As development goes on, though, we've found that the accumulated lore of the past few years is quite an entry barrier for new people. This book is a snapshot of the current status, designed to ease that first step. It covers the project through Apocalypse 6 and the 0.0.10 release of Parrot. Because Perl 6 is rapidly changing, we'll publish a revised edition of the book every year until Perl 6.0.0 is released.

How This Book Is Organized

This book has seven chapters:

- Chapter 1 is a high-level overview of the project, with some history of how and why the project was started.
- Chapter 2 provides more detail on life cycles within the project and how to get involved.
- Chapter 3 explains some of the principles behind Perl 6 design work.
- Chapter 4 is an introduction to Perl 6 syntax.
- Chapter 5 explains the overall architecture of Parrot (the virtual machine that runs Perl 6).

- Chapter 6 is an introduction to Parrot assembly language.
- Chapter 7 is an introduction to Parrot's Intermediate Code Compiler.

If you're a Perl programmer who is completely new to Perl 6, you'll be interested in this book to get an idea of what it'll be like to work with Perl 6, why we're making the changes we're making, and how the project is going. You'll want to read the first four chapters. If you think you might be interested in getting involved in implementation, read the rest as well.

If you're already involved in the Perl 6 project, you'll be interested in this book to see how all the pieces fit together, and you may want to use it as a reference while you're working. If you've been involved only on the language side or the internals side, you'll also get a chance to see what the other half is doing. In this way, the entire book is relevant to you.

If you're interested in implementing another language on top of Parrot, you'll want to skim through the Parrot information in Chapter 2, and then skip straight to Chapter 5 and read from there.

If you're not involved in Perl but just want to see what the "Perl 6" buzz is all about, you'll want to read Chapters 1, 3, and 5. You'll get an overview of what we're doing and why, without all the nitty-gritty details.

Font Conventions

The following font conventions are used in this book:

- *Italic* is used for filenames, URLs, and email addresses
- `Constant width` is used in code listings and for function names, variable names, and other literal text
- `Constant width italic` is used to indicate replaceable items in code

We'd Like to Hear from You

Please address comments and questions concerning this book to the publisher:

O'Reilly & Associates, Inc.
1005 Gravenstein Highway North
Sebastopol, CA 95472
(800) 998-9938 (in the United States or Canada)
(707) 829-0515 (international or local)
(707) 829-0104 (fax)

We have a web page for this book, where we list errata, examples, or any additional information. You can access this page at:

http://www.oreilly.com/catalog/perl6es

To comment or ask technical questions about this book, send email to:

bookquestions@oreilly.com

For more information about our books, conferences, Resource Centers, and the O'Reilly Network, see our web site at:

http://www.oreilly.com

Acknowledgments

We'd like to thank the reviewers who helped whip this book into shape: Damian Conway, David Hand, Luke Palmer, Joseph Ryan, and Randal Schwartz. Allison would also like to thank the University of Portland for its support of her work on this book and on Perl 6.

This book is dedicated to the Perl community, because it wouldn't exist without them.

## CHAPTER 1

Project Overview

*Conceptual integrity in turn dictates that
the design must proceed from one mind,
or from a very small number
of agreeing resonant minds.*
—Frederick Brooks Jr.
The Mythical Man Month

Perl 6 is the next major version of Perl. It's a complete rewrite of the interpreter, and a significant update of the language itself. The goal of Perl 6 is to add support for much-needed new features, and still be cleaner, faster, and easier to use.

The Perl 6 project is vast and complex, but it isn't complicated. The project runs on a simple structure with very little management overhead. That's really the only way it could run. The project doesn't have huge cash or time resources. Its only resource is the people who believe in the project enough to spend their off-hours—their "relaxation" time—working to see it completed. This chapter is as much about people as it is about Perl.

The Birth of Perl 6

Back on July 18, 2000, the second day of the fourth Perl Conference (TPC 4), a small band of Perl geeks gathered to prepare for a meeting of the Perl 5 Porters later that day. The topic at hand was the current state of the Perl community. Four months had passed since the 5.6.0 release of Perl, and although it introduced some important features, none were revolutionary.

There had been very little forward movement in the previous year. It was generally acknowledged that the Perl 5 codebase had grown difficult to maintain. At the same time, infighting on the *perl5-porters* list had grown so intense that some of the best developers decided to leave. It was time for a change, but no one was quite sure what to do. They started conservatively with plans to change the organization of Perl development.

An hour into the discussion, around the time most people nod off in any meeting, Jon Orwant (the reserved, universally respected editor of the Perl Journal) stepped quietly into the room and snapped everyone to attention with an entirely uncharacteristic and well-planned gesture. *Smash!* A coffee mug hit the wall. "We are *@$!-ed (*Crash!*) unless we can come up with something that will excite the community (*Pow!*), because everyone's getting bored and going off and doing other things! (*Bam!*)" (At least, that's basically how Larry tells it. As is usually the case with events like this, no one remembers exactly what Jon said.)

Awakened by this display, the group started to search for a real solution. The language needed room to grow. It needed the freedom to evaluate new features without the obscuring weight of legacy code. The community needed something to believe in, something to get excited about.

Within a few hours the group settled on Perl 6, a complete rewrite of Perl. The plan wasn't just a language change, just an implementation change, or just a social change. It was a paradigm shift. Perl 6 would be the community's rewrite of Perl, and the community's rewrite of itself.

Would Perl 6, particularly Perl 6 as a complete rewrite, have happened without this meeting? Almost certainly. The signs appeared on the lists, in conferences, and in journals months in advance. If it hadn't started that day, it would have happened a week later, or perhaps a few months later, but it would have happened. It was a step the community needed to take.

In the Beginning...

Let's pause and consider Perl development up to that fateful meeting. Perl 6 is just another link in the chain. The motivations behind it and the directions it will take are partially guided by history.

Perl was first developed in 1987 by Larry Wall while he was working as a programmer for Unisys. After creating a configuration and monitoring system for a network that spanned the two American coasts, he was faced with the task of assembling usable reports from log files scattered across the network. The available tools simply weren't up to the job. A linguist at heart, Larry set out to create his own programming language, which he called *perl*. He released the first version of Perl on December 18, 1987. He made it freely available on Usenet (this was before the Internet took over the world, remember), and quickly a community of Perl programmers grew.

The early adopters of Perl were system administrators who had hit the wall with shell scripting, *awk*, and *sed*. However, in the mid-1990s Perl's audience exploded with the advent of the Web, as Perl was tailor-made for CGI scripting and other web-related programming.

Meantime, the Perl language itself kept growing, as Larry and others kept adding new features. Probably the most revolutionary change in Perl (until Perl 6, of course) was the addition of packages, modules, and object-oriented programming with Perl 5. While this made the transition period from Perl 4 to Perl 5 unusually long, it breathed new life into the language by providing a modern, modular interface. Before Perl 5, Perl was considered simply a scripting language; after Perl 5, it was considered a full-fledged programming language.

Larry, meanwhile, started taking a back seat to Perl development and allowed others to take responsibility for adding new features and fixing bugs in Perl. The Perl 5 Porters (p5p) mailing list became the central clearinghouse for bug reports or proposed changes to the Perl language, with the "pumpkin holder" (also known as the "pumpking") being the programmer responsible for implementing the patches and distributing them to the rest of the list for review. Larry continued to follow Perl development, but like a parent determined not to smother his children, he stayed out of the day-to-day development, limiting his involvement to situations in which he was truly needed.

Although you might think that the birth of the Perl 6 project would be the first nail in the coffin for Perl 5, that's far from the case. If anything, Perl 5 has had a huge resurgence of development, with Perl 5.7.0 released only two weeks after the initial decision to go ahead with Perl 6. Perl 5.8, spearheaded by Jarkko Hietaniemi and released in July 2002, includes usable Unicode support, a working threads interface, safe signals, and a significant improvement of the internals with code cleanup, bug fixes, better documentation, and more than quadrupled test coverage. Hugo van der Sanden is the pumpking for 5.9–5.10. Plans for those releases include enhancements to the regular expression engine, further internals cleanup and a "use perl6ish" pragma that will integrate many of the features of Perl 6. Perl 5 is active and thriving, and will continue to be so even after the release of Perl 6.0.

The Continuing Mission

Much has changed since the early days of the project. New people join the group and others leave in a regular "changing of the guard" pattern. Plans change as the work progresses, and the demands of the work and the needs of the community become clearer. Today the Perl 6 project has three major parts: language design, internals, and documentation. Each branch is relatively autonomous, though there is a healthy amount of coordination between them.

Language Design

As with all things Perl, the central command of the language design process is Larry Wall, the creator of the Perl language. Larry is supported by the rest of the design team: Damian Conway, Allison Randal, Dan Sugalski, Hugo van der Sanden, and chromatic. We speak in weekly teleconferences and also meet face-to-face a few times a year to hash out ideas for the design documents, or to work through roadblocks standing in the way of design or implementation. The group is diverse, including programmers-for-hire, Perl trainers, and linguists with a broad spectrum of interests and experiences. This diversity has proved quite valuable in the design process, as each member is able to see problems in the design or potential solutions that the other members missed.

Requests for comments (RFCs)

The first step in designing the new language was the RFC (Request For Comments) process. This spurred an initial burst of community involvement. Anyone was free to submit an RFC on any subject, whether it was as small as adding an operator, or as big as reworking OO syntax. Most of the proposals were really quite conservative. The RFCs followed a standard format so they would be easier to read and easier to compare.

Each RFC was subject to peer review, carried out in an intense few weeks around October 2000. One thing the RFC process demonstrated was that the Perl community still wasn't quite ready to move beyond the infighting that had characterized Perl 5 Porters earlier that year.[*]

Even though few RFCs have been accepted without modification, the process identified a large number of irritants in the language. These have served as signposts for later design efforts.

---

[*] Mark-Jason Dominus wrote an excellent critique of the RFC process (*http://www.perl.com/pub/a/2000/11/perl6rfc.html*). It may seem harsh to people accustomed to the more open and tolerant community of today, but it's an accurate representation of the time when it was written.

Apocalypses and Exegeses

The Apocalypses* and Exegeses† are an important part of the design process. Larry started the Apocalypse series as a systematic way of answering the RFCs. Each Apocalypse corresponds to a chapter in his book *Programming Perl*, and addresses the features in the chapter that are likely to change.

However, the Apocalypses have become much more than a simple response to RFCs. Larry has a startling knack for looking at 12 solutions to a problem, pulling out the good bits from each one, and combining them into a solution that is 10 times better than any of the proposals alone. The Apocalypses are an excellent example of this "Larry Effect." He addresses each relevant RFC, and gives reasons why he accepted or rejected various pieces of it. But each Apocalypse also goes beyond a simple "yes" and "no" response to attack the roots of the problems identified in the RFCs.

Damian Conway's Exegeses are extensions of each Apocalypse. Each Exegesis is built around a practical code example that applies and explains the new ideas.

The p6l mailing list

The next body of design work is the Perl 6 Language mailing list (*perl6-language@perl.org*), often fondly referred to as "p6l." Luke Palmer has been deputized as unofficial referee of the list. He answers questions that don't require the direct involvement of the design team or that have been answered before. He also keeps an eye out for good suggestions to make sure the design team doesn't miss them in the sea of messages. The list has approximately 40 regular contributors in any given month, as well as a large number of occasional posters and lurkers. Some people have participated since the very beginning; others appear for a few months and move on.

Even though the individuals change, the general tone of p6l is the same. It's an open forum for any ideas on the user-visible parts of Perl 6. In the typical pattern, one person posts an idea and 5 to 10 people respond with criticisms or suggestions. The list periodically travels down a speculative thread like a runaway train, but these eventually run out of steam. Then Larry picks out the golden bits and gently tells the rest that no, he never intended Perl 6 to have hyper-vulcan mechanoid scooby-dooby-doos. Even when Larry doesn't post, he follows the list and the traffic serves as a valuable catalyst for his thoughts.

---

* An "apocalypse" in the sense of "revelation," not "end of the world."
† An "exegesis" is an explanation or interpretation of a text.

Internals

Parrot is a grandiose idea that turned out to be more realistic than anyone originally could have believed: why not have a single interpreter for several languages? Unlike the parent Perl 6 project, which was launched in a single day, the plan for Parrot formed in bits and pieces over the space of a year.

On April 1, 2001, Simon Cozens published an article titled "Programming Parrot" as an April Fools' joke (*http://www.perl.com/pub/a/2001/04/01/ parrot.htm*). It was a contrived interview with Larry Wall and Guido van Rossum detailing their plans to merge Python and Perl into a new language called Parrot. A few months later, when Perl 6 internals began to take an independent path within the larger project, they dubbed the subproject "Parrot" in a fitting turn of life imitating art.

Early Steps Toward Perl 6 Internals

The earliest progress toward implementing Perl 6 started before the current incarnation of Perl 6 was even conceived. The Topaz project, started in 1998, was spearheaded by Chip Salzenberg. It was a reimplementation of Perl 5 written in C++. The project was abandoned, but many of the goals and intended features for Topaz were adopted for Perl 6 internals, and the difficulties Topaz encountered were also valuable guides.

Sapphire was another early prototype that influenced the shape of Perl 6 internals. It was a one-week project in September 2000. The brainchild of Simon Cozens, Sapphire was another rewrite of Perl 5 internals. It was never intended for release, only as an experiment to see how far the idea could go in a week, and what lessons could be learned.

The plan for Parrot was to build a language-neutral runtime environment. It would support all the features of dynamic languages such as Python, Ruby, Scheme, Befunge, and others. It would have threading and Unicode support (two of the most problematic features to add into Perl 5 code) built in from the start. It would support exceptions and compilation to bytecode, and have clean extension and embedding mechanisms.

The language-neutral interpreter was originally just a side effect of good design. Keeping the implementation independent of the syntax would make the code cleaner and easier to maintain. One practical advantage of this design was that Parrot development could begin even though the Perl 6 language specification was still in flux.

The bigger win in the long term, though, was that since Parrot would support the features of the major dynamic languages and wasn't biased to a particular syntax, it could run all these languages with little additional effort. It's generally acknowledged that different languages are suited to different tasks. Picking which language will be used in a large software project is a common planning problem. There's never a perfect fit. It usually boils down to picking the language with the most advantages and the least noticeable disadvantages. The ability to combine multiple languages within a project could be a huge benefit. Use well-tested libraries from one language for one task. Take advantage of a clean way of expressing a particular problem domain in a second, without being forced to use it in areas where it's weak.

The modular design also benefits future language designers. Instead of targeting *lex/yacc* and reimplementing low-level features such as garbage collection and dynamic types, designers can write a parser that targets the Parrot virtual machine.

The internals development for Perl 6 falls to the Parrot project. Dan Sugalski leads the project as internals designer, and Steve Fink is the current pumpking. The Parrot project is largely autonomous. Dan coordinates with the rest of the design team to ensure that Parrot will be able to support the semantics Perl 6 will require, but the language designers have very little input into the details of implementation. Parrot isn't developed solely for Perl, but Perl 6 is entirely dependent on Parrot—it is the only interpreter for Perl 6.

The core communication line for the Parrot project is the mailing list, *perl6-internals@perl.org*, otherwise known as "p6i." It's a much more business-like list than p6l. Workflow in Parrot takes the form of submitted patches. Anyone is free to submit a patch, and contributors who consistently submit valuable patches over a long period of time are granted check-in access to the CVS repository.

Documentation

Though adequate documentation has been a goal from the very beginning, the Perl 6 documentation project is a relatively recent addition. It operates under the guidance of Michael Lazzaro. The stated goal of the documentation project is to systematically walk through each Apocalypse and produce fully specified documentation from it. The results of the project are eventually intended to be the documentation released with Perl 6.0.

The task of the documenters is a difficult one. The specification for Perl 6 is still in development and constantly shifting, so they're shooting at a moving target. The process is immensely valuable though, as it helps to identify inconsistencies or problems in the design that the broad brushstrokes of the Apocalypses miss. Sometimes it is the documentation process that causes the shift in language specification, as identified problems lead to solutions and the solutions, in turn, trigger changes throughout the system.

Supporting Structure

Last, but not least, is the glue that holds the project together. The highest praise belongs to Ask Björn Hansen and Robert Spier, who manage the email, revision control, and bug-tracking systems, as well as the web pages for Perl 6 and Parrot. Without these systems, the project would grind to a screeching halt.

Nathan Torkington and Allison Randal share the load of project management. Nat tends to handle outside interfacing while Allison tends to handle the nuts and bolts of the project, but neither role is set in stone. As is typical of open source development projects, managing the Perl 6 project is quite different from managing a commercial project of the same size and complexity. There are no schedules, no deadlines, no hiring and firing, and no salaries, bonuses, or stock options. There are no employees or bosses; there is very little hierarchy whatsoever. Management in this context isn't about giving orders, it's about making sure everyone has what they need to keep moving forward.

In the end, it is the developers themselves who hold the project together. Each individual bears their own share of the responsibility for finding a task that suits their skills, coordinating with others to keep duplicated effort minimal, and making sure the job gets done.

## CHAPTER 2

Project Development

*The culture's (and my own) understanding
of large projects that don't follow a
benevolent-dictator model is weak.
Most such projects fail. A few become
spectacularly successful and important
(Perl, Apache, KDE). Nobody really
understands where the difference lies.*

—Eric S. Raymond
The Cathedral and The Bazaar

The Perl community is rich and diverse. There are as many variations in skill sets and skill levels as there are people. Some are coders, some are testers, some are writers, some are teachers, some are theorists. For every skill, there is a task. It's the combination of all the skills that gets the job done. A team of workers all wielding hammers could never build a house. Someone has to cut the wood, sand it, apply plaster, paint it, and install windows, doors, electrical systems, and plumbing.

Language Development

Theoretically, language design is the driving force behind all other parts of the project. In actual practice, Parrot development and documentation frequently affect the direction and focus of design efforts. A design that gave no consideration to what can be implemented efficiently wouldn't be much use. Equally, if the design work followed a strictly linear path, it would be a waste of developer resources. The Parrot project can't afford to go on hold every time they need information from a future area of design. For example, the design of OO syntax hasn't been completed yet, but the design team took time to define enough of the required semantics so that development can move ahead.

Development Cycles

Design work goes in cycles. Each cycle begins with a quiet period. During this time, the list traffic is fairly light, and Larry is rarely seen. It can seem as if the project is stalled, but in fact, this part of the cycle is where the bulk of original design work is done. Larry disappears when he's working on an Apocalypse. It's the most intense and creative phase.

The next phase is internal revision. Larry sends a draft of the Apocalypse to the design team for comments and makes changes based on their suggestions. Sometimes the changes are as simple as typo fixes, but sometimes they entirely alter the shape of the design. Larry repeats this several times before publishing the document. This is a very fast-paced and dynamic phase, but again, low on visible results.

Next is the community review. Usually the first day or two after an Apocalypse comes out are quiet, while the ideas soak in. Then the list begins to fly. Some people suggest changes, while others ask about the design. This phase reflects the most visible progress, but the changes are mostly refinements. The changes introduced at community review polish off the rough edges, add a few new tricks, or make simplifications for the average user. Here the community takes ownership of the design, as both the design and the people change until the two are a comfortable fit. The Synopsis, a summary released by the design team soon after each Apocalypse, assists in the community review by breaking down the ideas from the Apocalypse into a simple list of points.

The Exegesis comes next, and its process is much like that of the Apocalypse. List traffic slows again while Damian writes and the design team revises. The Exegesis responds to the community review. The practical example at the core of each Exegesis explains the parts of the Apocalypse that were hardest to understand and fleshes out some of the holes found in the community review. The list bursts into another flurry of activity as the community reviews the Exegesis. Then the cycle starts all over again.

Getting Involved

The primary cycle of Apocalypses, Synopses, and Exegeses is not the only movement in design. Constant activity on and off the list packs around the larger cycle. Old decisions are revisited; future decisions are previewed.

Getting involved in Perl 6 design work is as simple, and as difficult, as joining the list. Subscribing to a list takes almost no effort, but the most valuable contributions don't come from people who respond to an idea here and there, though those are certainly welcome. The posts with the greatest impact come from people who take the time to learn the system—to figure out what Perl 6 is all about.

If you want to make a valuable contribution, get on the list and listen. Work to understand the issues behind each thread of discussion. Soon you'll find there are repetitions in the themes, guiding principles that shape the debates.

Form a mental map of the new syntax. It's not an easy task. There are no interpreters available for Perl 6, so if you forget how a particular feature works you can't just experiment. Mainly, you'll have to search through the list archives—over, and over, and over again. And the syntax keeps changing. You'll have a perfect grasp on a feature just before it changes. It can be frustrating, but it is well worth it.

Parrot Development

Parrot development is the productive core of Perl 6 development. If you want coding action, this is the place to be.

Organization of the Parrot project is lightweight but efficient. It's a meritocracy—people who make valuable contributions are offered more responsibility. Communication is relaxed and informal. As Dan is so fond of saying, "This is far too important to take seriously." It's a bit like a special forces unit—the work gets done not because of tight control from the top, but because the whole team knows what they need to do, and do it.

Development Cycles

The cycles in Parrot development center on "point releases." A point release is a version change, such as 0.0.8 to 0.0.9. The pumpking decides when point releases happen and what features are included. Usually one or two solid new features trigger a release.

Development proceeds at a steady pace of bug reports, patches submitted, and patches applied. The pace isn't so much a result of careful planning as it is the law of averages—on any given day, someone, somewhere, is working on Parrot. A release is a spike in that activity, but since Parrot tends to follow the "release early, release often" strategy, the spike is relatively small.

Typically, a few days before a release the pumpking declares a feature freeze and all development efforts center on bug squashing. This periodic cleanup is one of the most valuable aspects of a release.

Getting Involved

Just like design work, the first step to participating in Parrot development is joining the list. The topics on p6i tend to stick to practical matters: bug reports, patches, notifications of changes committed to CVS, and questions on coding style. Occasionally there are discussions about how to implement a particular feature. In general, if you have a question about syntax or a speculation about whether Perl 6 should support a particular feature, that question belongs on the language list rather than the internals list.

Use the source

The second step to participating in Parrot development is to get a copy of the source code. If you just want to try it out—experiment with a few features and see how it feels—you're probably best off downloading a tarball. For the most stable copy, grab the latest point release from CPAN. The sure way to get the most recent release is to search on *http://search.cpan.org* for "parrot" in "Distributions." If you want something a little more cutting edge than the packaged release, a new snapshot of the CVS repository is created every eight hours. The most recent snapshot is always available at *http://cvs. perl.org/snapshots/parrot/parrot-latest.tar.gz*.

If you plan to get involved in development, you'll want to check out the source from the CVS repository. Anyone can get anonymous access. Just log in as the "anonymous" user and check out the source. No password is necessary.

```
cvs -d :pserver:anonymous@cvs.perl.org:/cvs/public login
cvs -d :pserver:anonymous@cvs.perl.org:/cvs/public checkout parrot
```

There's also a web interface for viewing files in the repository at *http://cvs. perl.org/cvsweb/parrot/*.

Now that you've got the source, take a moment to look around. The code changes constantly, so a detailed description of every file is impossible. But a few road signs are helpful starting out.

The most important top-level directory is *docs/*. The content isn't always up to date, but it is a good place to start. *parrot.pod* provides a quick overview of what is in each documentation file.

The *languages/* directory contains the code that implements various language compilers: Perl 6, as well as Python, Ruby, Scheme, Befunge, BASIC, etc. Most are in various stages of partial completion. If you have a language you're particularly interested to see implemented on Parrot, you might take a peek to see how far along it is.

The *lib/* directory contains Perl 5 classes currently used in developing Parrot. The *classes/* directory contains the C source code for Parrot classes (PMCs, which you'll read more about in Chapter 6). *examples/* contains some example Parrot assembler code, as well as benchmarks.

For instructions on building Parrot, see Chapter 6.

Patch submission

Parrot development is a continuous stream of patches. Patches are the currency of exchange in the project—the unit of work. They fix bugs, add features, modify features, remove features, and improve the documentation. Pretty much anything that changes, changes via a patch.

While anyone is free to submit a patch, a small number of people have access to commit changes to the CVS repository. This system works well. It means the project can harness the efforts of a large group, but still keep the same high quality as a small group of experienced developers.

Every submitted patch is automatically forwarded to the p6i list where it's subject to peer review. Patches spark little debate. Parrot developers generally submit code that's clean and well thought-out, so there's rarely any need for debate. Also, patches are typically small modular changes, which makes them easy to evaluate. Occasionally an entire language implementation is submitted in a single patch, but these are the exceptions.

Submitting a patch is fairly straightforward. You create a file listing of all your changes and email it to the ticket tracking system at *bugs-parrot@bugs6.perl.org*. But a few common-sense guidelines will make your patches cleaner, better, and less likely to give the pumpking hives.

First off, create your patches from a checked-out CVS repository, not from a tarball, so your diff is running against the latest version of the files. Then, make sure the paths listed in the patch match those in the repository. There are two methods of creating patches that will do this for you. You can make changes directly in your checked-out copy of the CVS repository and then create diffs using cvs diff -u. Or you can make a copy of the repository and then create diffs between the two copies with the standard diff -u. For example:

```
diff -u parrot/README parrot_changed/README
```

Either method is fine, and both are equally common on p6i. Your working style and the types of changes you make—small and modular versus large and sweeping—will influence which method you choose.

Next, when you're making changes, take some extra time to consider how your patch affects the rest of the system. If your patch adds a new file, patch

the main *MANIFEST* file to include it. If you add a new feature, add a test
for it. If you fix a bug, add a test for it. See "Writing Tests" in Chapter 6 for
more on writing tests for Parrot. Before you submit a patch, always recom-
pile the system with your patch included and run all tests as follows:

```
make clean
perl Configure.pl
make
make test
```

Then consider the people who will review and apply your patch, and try to
make their jobs easier. Patch filenames should be as descriptive as possible:
fix_readme_typo.patch is better than *README.patch*. An attached file is better than a diff pasted into an email, because it can be applied without manual editing. The conventional extension for patch files is *.patch*.

In the email message, always start the subject with "[PATCH]", and make
the subject as clear as possible: "[PATCH] misspelled aardvark in main
README file" is better than "[PATCH] typo." The body of the message
should clearly explain what the patch is supposed to do and why you're submitting it. Make a note if you're adding or deleting files so they won't be
missed.

Here is a good example of a patch submission using the CVS diff method
(an actual patch from p6i). It's short, sticks to the point, and clearly
expresses the problem and the solution. The patch filename and the subject
of the message are both descriptive:

```
Subject: [PATCH] Pointers in List_chunk not initialized
From: Bruce Gray

On Win32, these tests are segfaulting due to invalid
pointers in List_chunk structs:
t/op/string.t           97-98
t/pmc/intlist.t         3-4
t/pmc/pmc.t             80

The problem is caused by list.c/allocate_chunk not
initializing the pointers. This patch corrects the problem.


--
Hope this helps,
Bruce Gray
```

With the attached file *list_chunk_initialize.patch*:

```
Index: list.c
================================================================
RCS file: /cvs/public/parrot/list.c,v
retrieving revision 1.23
diff -u -r1.23 list.c
```

```
--- list.c      27 Dec 2002 09:33:11 -0000       1.23
+++ list.c      28 Dec 2002 03:37:35 -0000
@@ -187,6 +187,10 @@
    Parrot_block_GC(interpreter);
    chunk = (List_chunk *)new_bufferlike_header(interpreter,
sizeof(*chunk));
    chunk->items = items;
+   chunk->n_chunks = 0;
+   chunk->n_items  = 0;
+   chunk->next     = NULL;
+   chunk->prev     = NULL;
    Parrot_allocate_zeroed(interpreter, (Buffer *)chunk, size);
    Parrot_unblock_DOD(interpreter);
    Parrot_unblock_GC(interpreter);
```

Bug tracking

Bug reports go to the same address as patch submissions (*bugs-parrot@bugs6.perl.org*). Similar conventions apply: make the subject and the message as clear and descriptive as possible. There's no set convention on subject lines, but you can't go wrong starting off with something like "[BUG]" or "[P6C BUG]" to make it immediately obvious what the message is about.

If you want to track a bug or patch you've submitted, the current queue of bugs and patches is publicly viewable at *http://bugs6.perl.org*. Bug tracking for Parrot is handled by the Request Tracker (RT) ticket tracking system from Best Practical Solutions.

CHAPTER 3
Design Philosophy

*Today's practicality is often no more than
the accepted form of yesterday's theory.*
—Kenneth Pike
  An Introduction to Tagmemics

At the heart of every language is a core set of ideals that give the language its direction and purpose. If you really want to understand the choices that language designers make—why they choose one feature over another or one way of expressing a feature over another—the best place to start is with the reasoning behind the choices.

Perl 6 has a unique set of influences. It has deep roots in Unix and the children of Unix, which gives it a strong emphasis on utility and practicality. It's grounded in the academic pursuits of computer science and software engineering, which gives it a desire to solve problems the right way, not just the most expedient way. It's heavily steeped in the traditions of linguistics and anthropology, which gives it the goal of comfortable adaptation to human use. These influences and others like them define the shape of Perl and what it will become.

Linguistic and Cognitive Considerations

Perl is a human language. Now, there are significant differences between Perl and languages like English, French, German, etc. For one, it is artificially constructed, not naturally occurring. Its primary use, providing a set of instructions for a machine to follow, covers a limited range of human existence. Even so, Perl is a language humans use for communicating. Many of the same mental processes that go into speaking or writing are duplicated in writing code. The process of learning to use Perl is much like learning to speak a second language. The mental processes involved in reading are also relevant. Even though the primary audience of Perl code is a machine, as often as not humans have to read the code while they're writing it, reviewing it, or maintaining it.

Many Perl design decisions have been heavily influenced by the principles of natural language. The following are some of the most important principles, the ones we come back to over and over again while working on the design and the ones that have had the greatest impact.

The Waterbed Theory of Complexity

The natural tendency in human languages is to keep overall complexity about equivalent, both from one language to the next, and over time as a language changes. Like a waterbed, if you push down the complexity in one part of the language, it increases complexity elsewhere. A language with a rich system of sounds (phonology) might compensate with a simpler syntax. A language with a limited sound system might have a complex way of building words from smaller pieces (morphology). No language is complex in every way, as that would be unusable. Likewise, no language is completely simple, as too few distinctions would render it useless.

The same is true of computer languages. They require a constant balance between complexity and simplicity. Restricting the possible operators to a small set leads to a proliferation of user-defined methods and subroutines. This is not a bad thing, in itself, but it encourages code that is verbose and difficult to read. On the other hand, a language with too many operators encourages code that is heavy in line noise and difficult to read. Somewhere in the middle lies the perfect balance.

The Principle of Simplicity

In general, a simple solution is preferable to a complex one. A simple syntax is easier to teach, remember, use, and read. But this principle is in constant tension with the waterbed theory. Simplification in the wrong area is one danger to avoid. Another is false simplicity or oversimplification. Some problems are complex and require a complex solution. Perl 6 grammars aren't simple. But they are complex at the language level in a way that allows simpler solutions at the user level.

The Principle of Adaptability

Natural languages grow and change over time. They respond to changes in the environment and to internal pressure. New vocabulary springs up to handle new communication needs. Old idioms die off as people forget them, and newer, more relevant idioms take their place. Complex parts of the system tend to break down and simplify over time. Change is what keeps language active and relevant to the people who use it. Only dead languages stop changing.

The plan for Perl 6 explicitly includes plans for future language changes. No one believes that Perl 6.0.0 will be perfect, but at the same time, no one wants another change process quite as dramatic as Perl 6. So Perl 6 will be flexible and adaptable enough to allow gradual shifts over time. This has influenced a number of design decisions, including making it easy to modify how the language is parsed, lowering the distinctions between core operations and user-defined operations, and making it easy to define new operators.

The Principle of Prominence

In natural languages, certain structures and stylistic devices draw attention to an important element. This could be emphasis, as in "The *dog* stole my wallet" (the dog, not the man), or extra verbiage, as in "It was the dog who stole my wallet," or a shift to an unusual word order, "My wallet was stolen by the dog" (my wallet, not my shoe, etc.), or any number of other verbal tricks.

Perl is designed with its own set of stylistic devices to mark prominence, some within the language itself, and some that give users flexibility to mark prominence within their code. The NAMED blocks use all capitals to draw attention to the fact that they're outside the normal flow of control. Perl 5 has an alternate syntax for control structures like if and for, which moves them to the end to serve as statement modifiers (because Perl is a left-to-right language, the left side is always a position of prominence). Perl 6 keeps this flexibility, and adds a few new control structures to the list.

The balance for design is to decide which features deserve to be marked as prominent, and where the syntax needs a little flexibility so the language can be more expressive.

The Principle of End Weight

Natural languages place large complex elements at the end of sentences. So, even though "I gave Mary the book" and "I gave the book to Mary" are equally comfortable, "I gave the book about the history of development of peanut-based products in Indonesia to Mary" is definitely less comfortable than the other way around. This is largely a mental parsing problem. It's easier to interpret the major blocks of the sentence all at once than to start with a few, work through a large chunk of minor information, and then go back to fill in the major sentence structure. Human memory is limited.

End weight is one of the reasons regular expression modifiers were moved to the front in Perl 6. It's easier to read a grammar rule when you know things like "this rule is case insensitive" right at the start. (It's also easier for the machine to parse, which is almost as important.)

End weight is also why there has been some desire to reorder the arguments in grep to:

```
grep @array { potentially long and complex block };
```

But that change causes enough cultural tension that it may not happen.

The Principle of Context

Natural languages use context when interpreting meaning. The meanings of "hot" in "a hot day," "a hot stereo," "a hot idea," and "a hot debate" are all quite different. The implied meaning of "it's wet" changes depending on whether it's a response to "Should I take a coat?" or "Why is the dog running around the kitchen?" The surrounding context allows us to distinguish these meanings. Context appears in other areas as well. A painting of an abstract orange sphere will be interpreted differently depending on whether the other objects in the painting are bananas, clowns, or basketball players. The human mind constantly tries to make sense of the universe, and it uses every available clue.

Perl has always been a context-sensitive language. It makes use of context in a number of different ways. The most obvious use is scalar and list contexts, where a variable may return a different value depending on where and how it's used. These have been extended in Perl 6 to include string context, boolean context, numeric context, and others. Another use of context is the $_ defaults, like print, chomp, matches, and now when.

Context-dependent features are harder to write an interpreter for, but they're easier on the people who use the language daily. They fit in with the way humans naturally think, which is one of Perl's top goals.

The Principle of DWIM

In natural languages there is a notion called "native speaker's intuition." Someone who speaks a language fluently will be able to tell whether a sentence is correct, even if they can't consciously explain the rules. (This has little to do with the difficulty English teachers have getting their students to use "proper" grammar. The rules of formal written English are very different from the rules of spoken English.)

As much as possible, features should do what the user expects. This concept of DWIM, or "Do What I Mean," is largely a matter of intuition. The user's experiences, language exposure, and cultural background all influence their expectations. This means that intuition varies from person to person. An English speaker won't expect the same things as a Dutch speaker, and an Ada programmer won't expect the same things as a COBOL programmer.

The trick in design is to use the programmer's intuitions instead of fighting against them. A clearly defined set of rules will never match the power of a feature that "just seems right."

Perl 6 targets Perl programmers. What seems right to one Perl programmer may not seem right to another, so no feature will please everyone. But it is possible to catch the majority cases.

Perl generally targets English speakers. It uses words like "given," which gives English speakers a head start in understanding its behavior in code. Of course, not all Perl programmers are English speakers. In some cases idiomatic English is toned down for broader appeal. In grammar rules, ordinal modifiers have the form 1st, 2nd, 3rd, 4th, etc., because those are most natural for native English speakers. But they also have an alternate form 1th, 2th, etc., with the general rule Nth, because the English endings for ordinal numbers are chaotic and unfriendly to non-native speakers.

The Principle of Reuse

Human languages tend to have a limited set of structures and reuse them repeatedly in different contexts. Programming languages also employ a set of ordinary syntactic conventions. A language that used { } braces to delimit loops but paired keywords to delimit if statements (like if ... then ... end if) would be incredibly annoying. Too many rules make it hard to find the pattern.

In design, if you have a certain syntax to express one feature, it's often better to use the same syntax for a related feature than to invent something entirely new. It gives the language an overall sense of consistency, and makes the new features easier to remember. This is part of why grammars are structured as classes.[*] Grammars could use any syntax, but classes already express many of the features grammars need, like inheritance and the concept of creating an instance.

The Principle of Distinction

The human mind has an easier time identifying big differences than small ones. The words "cat" and "dog" are easier to tell apart than "snore" and "shore." Usually context provides the necessary clues, but if "cats" were "togs," we would be endlessly correcting people who heard us wrong ("No, I said the Johnsons got a new dog, not tog, *dog*.").

The design consideration is to build in visual clues to subtle contrasts. The language should avoid making too many different things similar. Excessive overloading reduces readability and increases the chance for confusion. This is part of the motivation for splitting the two meanings of eval into try and eval, the two meanings of for into for and loop, and the two uses of sub into sub and method.

Distinction and reuse are in constant tension. If too many features are reused and overloaded, the language will begin to blur together. Far too much time will be spent trying to figure out exactly which use is intended. But, if too many features are entirely distinct, the language will lose all sense of consistency and coherence. Again, it's a balance.

Language Cannot Be Separated from Culture

A natural language without a community of speakers is a dead language. It may be studied for academic reasons, but unless someone takes the effort to preserve the language, it will eventually be lost entirely. A language adds to the community's sense of identity, while the community keeps the language relevant and passes it on to future generations. The community's culture shapes the language and gives it a purpose for existence.

Computer languages are equally dependent on the community behind them. You can measure it by corporate backing, lines of code in operation, or user interest, but it all boils down to this: a programming language is dead if it's not used. The final sign of language death is when there are no compilers or interpreters for the language that will run on existing hardware and operating systems.

---

[*] For more details on grammars, see "Grammars and Rules" in Chapter 4.

For design work this means it's not enough to only consider how a feature fits with other features in the language. The community's traditions and expectations also weigh in, and some changes have a cultural price.

The Principle of Freedom

In natural languages there is always more than one way to express an idea. The author or speaker has the freedom, and the responsibility, to pick the best phrasing—to put just the right spin on the idea so it makes sense to their audience.

Perl has always operated on the principle that programmers should have the freedom to choose how to express their code. It provides easy access to powerful features and leaves it to the individuals to use them wisely. It offers customs and conventions rather than enforcing laws.

This principle influences design in several ways. If a feature is beneficial to the language as a whole, it won't be rejected just because someone could use it foolishly. On the other hand, we aren't above making some features difficult to use, if they should be used rarely.

Another part of the design challenge is to build tools that will have many uses. No one wants a cookbook that reads like a Stephen King novel, and no one wants a one-liner with the elaborate structure of a class definition. The language has to be flexible to accommodate freedom.

The Principle of Borrowing

Borrowing is common in natural languages. When a new technology (food, clothing, etc.) is introduced from another culture, it's quite natural to adopt the original name for it. Most of the time borrowed words are adapted to the new language. In English, no one pronounces "tortilla," "lasagna," or "champagne" exactly as in the original languages. They've been altered to fit the English sound system.

Perl has always borrowed features, and Perl 6 will too. There's no shame in acknowledging that another language did an excellent job implementing a particular feature. It's far better to openly borrow a good feature than to pretend it's original. Perl doesn't have to be different just for the sake of being different. Most features won't be adopted without any changes, though. Every language has its own conventions and syntax, and many aren't compatible. So, Perl borrows features, but uses equivalent structures to express them.

Architectural Considerations

The second set of principles governs the overall architecture of Perl 6. These principles are connected to the past, present, and future of Perl, and define the fundamental purpose of Perl 6. No principle stands alone; each is balanced against the others.

Perl Should Stay Perl

Everyone agrees that Perl 6 should still be Perl, but the question is, what exactly does that mean? It doesn't mean Perl 6 will have exactly the same syntax. It doesn't mean Perl 6 will have exactly the same features. If it did, Perl 6 would just be Perl 5. So, the core of the question is what makes Perl "Perl"?

True to the original purpose

Perl will stay true to its designer's original intended purpose. Larry wanted a language that would get the job done without getting in his way. The language had to be powerful enough to accomplish complex tasks, but still lightweight and flexible. As Larry is fond of saying, "Perl makes the easy things easy and the hard things possible." The fundamental design philosophy of Perl hasn't changed. In Perl 6, the easy things are a little easier and the hard things are more possible.

Familiarity

Perl 6 will be familiar to Perl 5 users. The fundamental syntax is still the same. It's just a little cleaner and a little more consistent. The basic feature set is still the same. It adds some powerful features that will probably change the way we code in Perl, but they aren't required.

Learning Perl 6 will be like American English speakers learning Australian English, not English speakers learning Japanese. Sure, there are some vocabulary changes, and the tone is a little different, but it is still—without any doubt—English.

Translatable

Perl 6 will be mechanically translatable from Perl 5. In the long term, this isn't nearly as important as what it will be like to write code in Perl 6. But during the transition phase, automatic translation will be important. It will allow developers to start moving ahead before they understand every subtle nuance of every change. Perl has always been about learning what you need now and learning more as you go.

Important New Features

Perl 6 will add a number of features such as exceptions, delegation, multi-method dispatch, continuations, coroutines, and currying, to name a few. These features have proven useful in other languages and provide a great deal of power for solving certain problems. They improve the stability and flexibility of the language.

Many of these features are traditionally difficult to understand. Perl takes the same approach as always: provide powerful tools, make them easy to use, and leave it up to the user to decide whether and how to use them. Most users probably won't even know they're using currying when they use the assuming method.

Features like these are an important part of preparing Perl for the future. Who knows what development paradigms might develop in a language that has this combination of advanced features in a form easily approachable by the average programmer. It may not be a revolution, but it's certainly evolution.

Long-Term Usability

Perl 6 isn't a revision intended to last a couple of years and then be tossed out. It's intended to last 20 years or more. This long-range vision affects the shape of the language and the process of building it. We're not interested in the latest fad or in whipping up a few exciting tricks. We want strong, dependable tools with plenty of room to grow. And we're not afraid to take a little extra time now to get it right. This doesn't mean Perl 6.0 will be perfect, any more than any other release has been perfect. It's just another step of progress.

## CHAPTER 4

Syntax

*Language serves not only to express thought
but to make possible thoughts
which could not exist without it.*

—Bertrand Russell

Perl 6 is a work in progress, so the syntax is rapidly changing. This chapter is likely to be outdated by the time you read it. Even so, it provides a good baseline. If you start here, you'll only have to catch up on a few months of changes (starting with the design documents after Apocalypse 6), instead of several years worth.

Pretend for a moment that you don't know anything about Perl. You heard the language has some neat features, so you thought you might check it out. You go to the store and pick up a copy of *Programming Perl* because you think this Larry Wall guy might know something about it. It's the latest version, put out for the 6.0.1 release of Perl. It's not a delta document describing the changes, it's an introduction, and you dive in with the curiosity of a kid who got a telescope for his birthday. This chapter is a first glimpse down that telescope.

There's plenty of time later to analyze each feature and decide which you like and which you don't. For now, take a step back and get a feel for the system as a whole, for what it'll be like to work in it.

Variables

The most basic building blocks of a programming language are its nouns, the blobs of data that get sucked in, pushed around, altered in various ways, and spat out to some new location. The blobs of data are values: strings, numbers, etc., or composites of the simpler values. Variables are just named containers for those values. The three kinds of variables in Perl 6 are scalars, arrays, and hashes. Each has an identifying symbol (or sigil) as part of the name of the variable: $ for scalars, @ for arrays, and % for hashes. The sigils provide a valuable visual distinction by making it immediately obvious what kinds of behavior a particular variable is likely to have. But, fundamentally, there's little difference between the three. Each variable is essentially a container for a value, whether that value is single or collective. (This statement is an oversimplification, as you'll soon see.)

Scalars

Scalars are all-purpose containers. They can hold strings, integers, floating-point numbers, and references to all kinds of objects and built-in types. For example:

```
$string = "Zaphod's just this guy, you know?";
$int = 42;
$float = 3.14159;
$arrayref = [ "Zaphod", "Ford", "Trillian" ];
$hashref = { "Zaphod" => 362, "Ford" => 1574, "Trillian" => 28 };
$subref = sub { print $string };
$object = Android.new;
```

A filehandle is just an ordinary object in an ordinary scalar variable. For example:

```
$filehandle = open $filename;
```

Arrays

Array variables hold simple ordered collections of scalar values. Individual values are retrieved from the array by numeric index. The "0" index holds the first value. The @ sigil is part of the name of the variable and stays the same no matter how the variable is used:

```
@array = ( "Zaphod", "Ford", "Trillian" );

$second_element = @array[1]; # Ford
```

To get the length of an array—that is, the number of elements in an array—use the .length method. The .last method returns the index of the last element in an array—that is, the highest index in an array.

```
$count_elements = @array.length;
$last_index = @array.last;
```

Hashes

Hashes are unordered collections of scalar values, stored and retrieved by a key index. The simplest way to build a hash is by passing it a list of anonymous pair objects. These are formed with the pair constructor =>. For example:

```
%hash = ( "Zaphod" => 362, "Ford" => 1574, "Trillian" => 28 );
```

The key for each value may be a string or an object, though there are some restrictions on object keys. Hashes that use object keys must be declared as such, for the sake of efficiency.*

```
$age = %hash{"Zaphod"}; # string
$age = %hash{$name};    # string variable
$age = %hash{$person};  # object
```

In list context, a hash returns a list of key/value pair objects. The .kv method returns a flattened list of keys and values from a hash. So the assignment of a hash directly to an array:

```
@pairs = %hash;
```

breaks down into a list roughly equivalent to:

```
(pair1, pair2, pair3, etc...)
```

While the assignment of the flattened key/value list:

```
@flat = %hash.kv;
```

is roughly equivalent to:

```
(key1, value1, key2, value2, etc...)
```

The .keys method returns a flattened list of all the keys in a hash. The .values method returns a flattened list of all the values:

```
@keys = %hash.keys;
@values = %hash.values;
```

References

References are largely transparent in Perl 6. There is a distinction between references and ordinary variables, but it's minimized as much as possible in actual use, with automatic referencing and dereferencing where appropriate. Creating a reference to an array or hash requires no special syntax. You simply assign it to a scalar variable:

```
$arrayref = @array;
$hashref = %hash;
```

---

* Any object used as a hash key must have a .id method that returns a unique value for each unique object to avoid hashing collisions. This method is provided by default in the universal base class, so you only have to worry about uniqueness when you define your own .id methods.

References are implicitly dereferenced in many contexts, so array indexes and hash keys access individual elements directly from hashrefs and arrayrefs, just like they do with hashes and arrays:

```
$arrayref[1]
$hashref{"Zaphod"}
```

Methods are called on arrayrefs and hashrefs just like they are on arrays and hashes. The referent—the underlying data type or object—determines which methods can be used with a particular reference and whether it can support indexed access:

```
$arrayref.length
$hashref.kv
```

References to subroutines can be executed simply by passing the reference an argument list. The list can be empty, but the parentheses are required:

```
$subref($arg);
```

Arrayrefs and hashrefs have special syntax (@{...} and %{...}) for dereferencing them in structures that normally wouldn't.

Variables and Context

The primary difference between variables with the $ sigil and variables with @ or % sigils is that they each impose a different context. The $ sigil imposes a scalar context, @ imposes list context, and % imposes hashlist context.*

Scalar context

Any array or list evaluated in scalar context returns an arrayref. This means that assigning an array:

```
@array = ( "Zaphod", "Ford", "Trillian" );
$arrayref = @array;
```

a list:

```
$arrayref = ( "Zaphod", "Ford", "Trillian" );
```

or an explicit anonymous arrayref:

```
$arrayref = [ "Zaphod", "Ford", "Trillian" ];
```

to a scalar variable all produce exactly the same structure: a reference to an array with three elements.

---

* These three are not the only contexts in Perl 6. A complete discussion of Perl 6 contexts appears in "Operators" later in this chapter.

A single element in parentheses is not a list. The comma is the list constructor. Parentheses only group.* So when a one-element list is assigned in scalar context, it stays a simple scalar value:

```
$value = (20);
```

If you want to create an arrayref of one element in scalar context, use square
brackets ([...]) to explicitly construct an anonymous array reference:

```
$arrayref = [20];
```

Again, because a list in scalar context is an arrayref, a hash-like list assigned
to a scalar variable is simply a reference to an ordered array of pairs:

```
$pair_list = ( "Zaphod" => 362, "Ford" => 1574, "Trillian" => 28 );
```

You have to use curly braces ({...}) to explicitly construct a hash reference
in scalar context:

```
$hashref = { "Zaphod" => 362, "Ford" => 1574, "Trillian" => 28 };
```

List context

Variables with the @ sigil impose flattening list context. This means that if
you assign one array to another array, the original array is "flattened"—
treated as if it were a simple list of values—and every element from the original array is copied to the new array. The result is that the two array variables contain entirely different data structures, each with identical values:

```
@copy = @original;
```

A single value in list context is a one-element list, so it produces a one-element array on assignment:

```
@array = (20);
@array = 20;    # same
```

The anonymous arrayref constructor [...] imposes flattening list context
internally, but prevents flattening from outside. In scalar context, a simple
list and an arrayref construct produce the same result. But in list context, a
simple list is treated as a flattened list, while an arrayref construct is treated
as a list of one element, an arrayref:

```
@array = ( "Zaphod", "Ford", "Trillian" );
@array = [ "Zaphod", "Ford", "Trillian" ];
```

The first example above produces an array with three elements, while the
second produces an array with one element and that element is a reference

---

* One thread on p6l suggested parentheses as list constructors. This formulation has an unexpected
effect in structures that use parentheses for grouping: $val = 10 / (2 + 3) is the value "2", while
$val = (10 / (2 + 3)) is an array reference with a single element "2".

to an array with three elements. This is useful for building up complex data structures where simple values alternate with array references:

```
@array = ( "Marvin", [ "Zaphod", "Ford", "Trillian" ], "Zarniwoop" );
```

Similarly, in flattening list context a list of array variables are flattened into a single array, while a list of scalar variables are treated as a simple list, even if the scalar variables are arrayrefs. So, the first example produces an array containing all the elements of the three arrays, while the second produces an array of three arrayrefs:

```
@array = ( @array1, @array2, @array3 ); # single flattened list
@array = ( $arrayref1, $arrayref1, $arrayref3 ); # 3 element list
```

A lone pair of parentheses is a special token meaning "empty list." It produces an array structure with no elements in both scalar and list context:

```
$arrayref = ( );
@array = ( );
```

Hashlist context

Variables with % sigils impose hashlist context, which expects a list of pair objects. This is typically simply a list of anonymous pairs built with the pair constructor, =>, as follows:

```
%hash = ( "Zaphod" => 362, "Ford" => 1574, "Trillian" => 28 );
```

Equally, in hashlist context a list of simple values is treated as a list of pairs. Note that this substitution of two values for a pair object is only possible in hashlist context:

```
%hash = ( "Zaphod", 362, "Ford", 1574, "Trillian", 28 );
```

Curly braces {...} are the anonymous hash reference constructor, but they don't impose hashlist context. This is because curly braces alone assigned to a scalar variable define an anonymous subroutine:

```
# a sub reference that does nothing
$subref = { "Zaphod", 362, "Ford", 1574, "Trillian", 28 };
```

You can't use commas in place of pair constructors when assigning a hash reference to a scalar variable, because it's the => that marks the structure as a hash. So, the hash reference constructor isn't really {...}, but {... => ...}. If there's ever any ambiguity, you can also force the right context by specifying hash or sub before the block:

```
$subref = sub { print "Lost luggage.\n"; }
$hashref = hash { "Zaphod", 362, "Ford", 1574, "Trillian", 28 };
```

Properties and Traits

Properties allow additional information to be attached to variables and values. As Damian likes to explain it, they're much like sticky notes. You can take a note, scribble some important information on it, and slap it onto the refrigerator, your monitor, or the dashboard of your car. When you're done, you peel it off and throw it away.

Some properties are attached at compile time. These are known as "traits." Traits are still properties, just a particular kind of property. Traits are fixed to the variable when it is declared and cannot be changed later. Compile-time traits are set with the is keyword:

```
my $pi is constant = 3.14159;
```

The constant trait specifies that the value of the variable can't be changed.

Other properties are attached at runtime. They may modify only values, not variables. They can be added and removed at any time during the execution of the code. Runtime properties are set with the but keyword:

```
$true_value = 0 but true;
```

The true property specifies that the value will always evaluate as true, no matter what it is. This particular property means the Perl 6 system call can be checked with a simple conditional. It still returns the same numeric values it always has (0 on success and a numeric error code on failure), but it flags the value with a property as true when the call succeeds and false when it fails.

Internally, properties and traits are stored in hash-like structures with the property name as the key. Both constant and true define their own values when they're set. Some properties take arguments for their value:

```
my @array is dim(2,5,42);
```

Properties have proven to be an incredibly useful and extensible syntax. You'll see them again and again throughout this chapter. They aren't restricted to variables and values, but appear on subroutines, methods, classes, grammars, rules, and in parameter lists.

Types

The most important thing to understand about the Perl 6 type system is that it's completely optional. If you choose to use it, you'll gain some benefits in optimization and interfacing between languages. The type system isn't fully defined, but the basic groundwork is in place.

Perl 6 makes a distinction between the type of a value and the type of a variable. A value type specifies what kind of values a variable can hold. Putting an Int type on a scalar says that the scalar holds an integer value:

```
my Int $scalar;
```

Putting an Int type on an array says that the array holds integer values:

```
my Int @array;
```

And putting an Int type on a hash says that the hash holds integer values:

```
my Int %hash;
```

The variable type specifies what kind of container the variable is. This is basically like a tie in Perl 5. Variable types are defined as traits of the variable, with the is keyword. The sigils define an implicit variable type, so a variable with no type is just:

```
my $scalar is Scalar;
my @array is Array;
my %hash is Hash;
```

Hierarchical data structures can have a complex value type. A hash that holds integer arrays:

```
my Array of Int %hash;
```

has the value type Array of Int. The type syntax is flexible, so you could also write that as:

```
my %hash is Hash of Array of Int;
```

and get the same data structure. This improves readability, especially in multilevel data structures:

```
my Array of Hash of Array of Int %hash;
my %hash is Hash of Array of Hash of Array of Int;
```

Operators

Operators provide a simple syntax for manipulating values. Many of the Perl 6 operators will be familiar, especially to Perl programmers.

Assignment and Binding

The = operator is for ordinary assignment. It creates a copy of the values on the right-hand side and assigns them to the variables or data structures on the left-hand side:

```
$copy = $original;
@copies = @originals;
```

$copy and $original both have the same value, and @copies has a copy of every element in @originals.

The := operator is for binding assignment. Instead of copying the value from one variable or structure to the other, it creates an alias. An alias is an additional entry in the symbol table with a different name for the one container:

```
$a := $b;   # $a and $b are aliases
@c := @d;   # @c and @d are aliases
```

In this example, any change to $a also changes $b, because they're just two separate names for the same container. Binding assignment requires the same number of elements on both sides, so both of these would be an error:

```
# ($a, $b) := ($c);          # error
# ($a, $b) := ($c, $d, $e);  # error
```

The ::= operator is a variant of the binding operator that binds at compile time.

Arithmetic Operators

The binary arithmetic operators are addition (+), subtraction (-), multiplication (*), division (/), modulus (%), and exponentiation (**). Each has a corresponding assignment operator (+=, -=, *=, /=, %=, **=) that combines the arithmetic operation with assignment:

```
$a = 3 + 5;
$a += 5;    # $a = $a + 5
```

The unary arithmetic operators are the prefix and postfix autoincrement (++) and autodecrement (--) operators. The prefix operators modify their argument before it's evaluated, and the postfix operators modify it afterward:

```
$a++;
$a--;
++$a;
--$a;
```

String Operators

The ~ operator concatenates strings. The corresponding ~= operator concatenates the right-hand side of the assignment to the end of the string:

```
$line = "The quick brown " ~ $fox ~ jumps_over() ~ " the lazy " ~ $dog;
$line ~= "Belgium"; # adds to the string
```

The x operator replicates strings. It always returns a string no matter whether the left side of the operation is a single element or a list. The following example assigns the string "LintillaLintillaLintilla":

```
$triplet = "Lintilla" x 3;
```

The corresponding x= operator replicates the original string and assigns it back to the original variable:

```
$twin = "Lintilla";
$twin x= 2;          # "LintillaLintilla"
```

The xx operator replicates lists. It returns a list no matter whether it operates on a list of elements or a single element. The following example assigns a list of three elements to @array, each with the value "Lintilla":

```
@array = "Lintilla" xx 3;
```

The corresponding xx= operator creates a list that contains the specified number of copies of every element in the original array and assigns it back to the array variable:

```
@array xx= 2; # twice as many elements
@array = (@array, @array); # equivalent
```

Comparison

Each comparison operator has two forms, one for numeric comparisons and one for string comparisons. The comparison operators are greater-than (>, gt), less-than (<, lt), greater-than-or-equal (>=, ge), less-than-or-equal (<=, le), equality (==, eq), and inequality (!=, ne). Each returns a true value if the relation is true and a false value otherwise. The generic comparison operator (<=>, cmp) returns 0 if the two arguments are equal, 1 if the first is greater, and -1 if the second is greater.

Logical Operators

The binary logical operators test two values and return one value or the other depending on certain truth conditions. They're also known as the short-circuit operators because the right-hand side will never be evaluated if the overall truth value can be determined from the left-hand side. This makes them useful for conditionally assigning values or executing code.

The AND relation has the && operator and the low-precedence and operator. If the left-hand side is false, its value is returned. If the left-hand value is true, the right-hand side is evaluated and its value is returned:

```
$splat = $whale && $petunia;
$splat = ($whale and $petunia);
```

The OR relation has the || operator and the low-precedence or operator. The left-hand value is returned if it is true, otherwise the right-hand value is evaluated and returned:

```
$splat = $whale || $petunia;
$splat = ($whale or $petunia);
```

A variant of the OR relation tests for definedness instead of truth. It uses the // operator and the low-precedence err operator. The left-hand value is returned if it is defined, otherwise the right-hand side is evaluated and its value returned:

```
$splat = $whale // $petunia;
$splat = ($whale err $petunia);
```

The XOR relation has the ^^ operator and the low-precedence xor operator. It returns the value of the true operand if any one operand is true and a false value if both are true or neither is true. xor isn't short-circuiting like the others, because it always has to evaluate both arguments to know if the relation is true:

```
$splat = $whale ^^ $petunia;
$splat = ($whale xor $petunia);
```

Perl 6 also has boolean variants of the logical operators: ?& (AND), ?| (OR), and ?^ (XOR). These always return a true or false value.

Context Forcing Operators

The context of an expression specifies the type of value it is expected to produce. An array expects to be assigned multiple values at the same time, so assignment to an array happens in "list" context. A scalar variable expects to be assigned a single value, so assignment to a scalar happens in "scalar" context. Perl expressions often adapt to their context, producing values that fit with what's expected.

Contexts have proven to be valuable tools in Perl 5, so Perl 6 has a few more added. Void context still exists. Scalar context is subdivided into boolean, integer, numeric, string, and object contexts. Aside from flattening list context and hashlist context, which we mentioned earlier, list context is further subdivided into non-flattening list context and lazy list context.

Void context
    Expects no value.

Scalar context
    Expects a single value. Composite values are automatically referenced in scalar context.

Boolean context
    Expects a true or false value. This includes the traditional definitions of truth—where 0, undef, and the empty string are false and all other values are true—and values flagged with the properties true or false.

Numeric context
> Expects a number, whether it's an integer or floating-point, and whether it's decimal, binary, octal, hex, or some other base.

Integer context
> Expects an integer value. Strings are treated as numeric and floating-point numbers are truncated.

String context
> Expects a string value. It interprets any information passed to it as a string of characters.

Object context
> Expects an object, or more specifically, a reference to an object.

List context
> Expects a collection of values. Any single value in list context is treated as a one-element list.

Non-flattening list context
> Expects a list of objects. It treats arrays, hashes, and other composite values as discrete entities.

Flattening list context
> Expects a list, but flattens out arrays and hashes into their component parts.

Hashlist context
> Expects a list of pairs. A simple list in hashlist context pairs up alternating elements.

Lazy list context
> Expects a list, just like non-flattening list context, but doesn't require all the elements at once.

The unary context operators force a particular context when it wouldn't otherwise be imposed. Most of the time the default context is the right one, but at times you might want a little more control.

The unary ? operator and the low-precedence true force boolean context. Assignment of a scalar to a scalar only imposes generic scalar context, so the value of $number is simply copied. With the ? operator, you can force boolean context and assign the truth value of the variable instead of the numeric value:

```
$value = $number;
$truth = ?$number;
```

The unary ! operator and the low-precedence not also force boolean context, but they negate the value at the same time. They're often used in a boolean context, where only the negating effect is visible:

```
$untruth = !$number;
```

The unary + operator forces numeric context, and - forces negative numeric context:

```
$number = +$string;
$negnum = -$string;
```

The unary ~ operator forces string context:

```
$string = ~$number;
```

Bitwise Operators

Perl 6 has two sets of bitwise operators, one for integers and one for strings. The integer bitwise operators are +&, +|, and +^. Notice the combination of the AND, OR, and XOR relation symbols with the general numeric symbol + (the unary numeric context operator). There are also the numeric bitwise shift operators << and >>.

The string bitwise operators are ~&, ~|, and ~^. These combine the AND, OR, and XOR relation symbols with the general string symbol ~ (the same symbol as string concatenation and the unary string context operator).

Each of the bitwise operators has an assignment counterpart +&=, +|=, +^=, <<=, >>=, ~&=, ~|=, and ~^=.

Conditional

The ternary ??:: operator evaluates either its second or third operand, depending on whether the first operand evaluates as true or false. It's basically an if-then-else statement acting as an expression:

```
$form = ($heads == 2) ?? "Zaphod" :: "ape-descended lifeform";
```

Vector Operators

The vector operators are designed to work with lists. They're simply modified versions of the standard scalar operators. Every operator has a vectorized version, even user-defined operators. They have the same basic forms as their scalar counterparts, but are marked with the bracketing characters » and «,* or their plain-text equivalents >> and <<. So, the vectorized addition operator is >>+<<. Vector operators impose list context on their operands and distribute their operations across all the operands' elements. Vector

---

* These are the Unicode RIGHT POINTING GUILLEMET (U+00BB) and LEFT POINTING GUILLEMET (U+00AB) characters.

addition takes each element from the first list and adds it to the corresponding element in the second list:

```
@sums = @first >>+<< @second;
```

The resulting array contains the sums of each pair of elements, as if each pair were added with the scalar operator:

```
@sums = ( (@first[0] + @second[0]), (@first[1] + @second[1]), etc...);
```

If one side of a vector operation is a simple scalar, it is distributed across the list as if it were a list of identical elements:

```
@sums = @numbers >>+<< 5;
```

```
@sums ( (@numbers[0] + 5), (@numbers[1] + 5), etc... );
```

Junctions

At the simplest level, junction operators are no more than AND, OR, XOR, and NOT for values instead of expressions. The binary junction operators are & (AND), | (OR), and ^ (XOR).* So while || is a logical operation on two expressions:

```
if ($value == 1) || ($value == 2) { ... }
```

| is the same logical relation between two values:

```
if ($value == 1 | 2) { ... }
```

In fact, those two examples have exactly the same result: they return true when $value is 1 or 2 and false otherwise. In the common case that's all you'll ever need to know.

But junctions are a good deal more powerful than that, once you learn their secrets. In scalar context, a junctive operation doesn't return an ordinary single value, it returns a composite value containing all of its operands. This return value is a junction, and it can be used anywhere a junction operation is used:

```
$junc = 1 | 2;
if ($value == $junc) { ... }
```

Here, the variable $junc is used in place of 1 | 2, and has exactly the same effect as the earlier example.

A junction is basically just an unordered set with a logical relation defined between its elements. Any operation on the junction is an operation on the

---

* There isn't an operator for junctive NOT, but there is a function, as you'll see shortly.

entire set. Table 4-1 shows the way the four different types of junctions interact with other operators.

Table 4-1. Junctions

Function	Operator	Relation	Meaning
all	&	AND	Operation must be true for all values.
any	|	OR	Operation must be true for at least one value.
one	^	XOR	Operation must be true for exactly one value.
none		NOT	Operation must be false for all values.

The simplest possible example is the result of evaluating a junction in boolean context. The operation on the set is just "is it true?" This operation on an all junction is true if *all* the values are true:

```
true( $a & $b )
true( all($a,$b) )
```

So, if $a and $b are both true, the result is true.

On an any junction, it's true if *any* one value is true:

```
true( $a | $b )
true( any($a,$b) )
```

So, if $a or $b is true or if both are true, the result is true.

On a one junction, it's true only if exactly *one* value is true:

```
true( $a ^ $b )
true( one($a,$b) )
```

So, if either $a or $b is true, the result is true. But, if $a and $b are both true or neither is true, the result is false.

On a none junction, it's true only when *none* of the values are true—that is, when all the values are false.

```
true( none($a,$b) )
```

So, if $a and $b are both false, the result is true.

Ordinary arithmetic operators interact with junctions much like vector operators on arrays. A junction distributes the operation across all of its elements:

```
$junc = any(1, 2);
$junc += 5; # $junc is now any(6, 7)
```

Junctions can be combined to produce compact and powerful logical comparisons. If you want to test that two sets have no intersection, you might do something like:

```
if all($a, $b) == none($c, $d) { ... }
```

which tests that all of the elements of the first set are equal to none of the elements of the second set. Translated to ordinary logical operators that's:

```
if ($a != $c) && ($a != $d) && ($b != $c) && ($b != $d) { ... }
```

If you want to get back a flat list of values from a junction, use the .values method:

```
$junc = all(1, 2, 3);      # create a junction
$sums = $junc + 3;         # add 3
@set  = $sums.values();    # (4, 5, 6)
```

The .dump method returns a string that shows the structure of a junction:

```
$string = $sums.dump(); # "all(4,5,6)"
```

The .pick method selects one value from an any junction or a one junction that has exactly one value, and returns it as an ordinary scalar:

```
$junc = any(1, 2, 3);
$single = $junc.pick();  # may be 1, 2, or 3
```

On an all junction, a none junction, or a one junction with more than one value, .pick returns undef.*

Smart Match

The binary ~~ operator makes a smart match between its two terms. It returns a true value if the match is successful and a false value if the match fails.† The negated smart match operator !~ does the exact opposite: it returns true if the match fails and false if it is successful. The kind of match a smart match does is determined by the kind of arguments it matches. If the types of the two arguments can't be determined at compile time, the kind of match is determined at runtime. In all but two cases smart match is a symmetric operator, so you can reverse A ~~ B to B ~~ A and it will have the same truth value.

Matching scalars

Any scalar value or any code that results in a scalar value matched against a string tests for string equality. The following match is true if $string has the value "Ford":

```
$string ~~ "Ford"
```

---

* With some levels of error strictness, it may raise an exception.

† This is an oversimplification. Some matches return a more complex value, but in boolean context it will always evaluate as true for a successful match, and false for a failed match.

Any scalar value matched against a numeric value tests for numeric equality. The following is true if $number has the numeric value 42, or the string value "42":

```
$number ~~ 42
```

An expression that results in the value 42 is also true:

```
( (5 * 8) + 2 ) ~~ 42
```

Any scalar value matched against an undefined value checks for definedness. The following matches are true if $value is an undefined value and false if $value is any defined value:

```
$value ~~ undef
$value ~~ $undefined_value
```

Any scalar value matched against a rule (regex) does a pattern match. The following match is true if the sequence "towel" can be found anywhere within $string:

```
$string ~~ /towel/
```

Any scalar value matched against a substitution does that substitution on the value. This means the value has to be modifiable. The following match is true if the substitution succeeds on $string and false if it fails:

```
$string ~~ s/weapon/towel/
```

Any scalar value matched against a boolean value simply takes the truth value of the boolean. The following match will always be true, because the boolean on the right is always true:[*]

```
$value ~~ (1 == 1)
```

The boolean value on the right must be an actual boolean: the result of a boolean comparison or operation, the return value of a not or true function, or a value forced into boolean context by ! or ?. The boolean value also must be on the right; a boolean on the left is treated as an ordinary scalar value.

Matching lists

Any scalar value matched against a list compares each element in sequence. The match is true if at least one the element of the list would match in a simple expression-to-expression match. The following match is true if $value is the same as any of the three strings on the right:

```
$value ~~ ( "Zaphod", "Ford", "Trillian" )
```

---

[*] At the moment this relation won't seem particularly useful. It makes much more sense when you realize that the switch statement duplicates all the smart match relations. More on that in "The switch statement" later in this chapter.

This match is short-circuiting. It stops after the first successful match. It has the same truth value as a series of or-ed matches:

```
($value ~~ "Zaphod") or ($value ~~ "Ford") or ($value ~~ "Trillian")
```

A list can contain any combination of elements: scalar values, rules, boolean expressions, arrays, hashes, etc.:

```
$value ~~ ( "Zaphod", 5, /petunias/ )
```

A match of a list against another list sequentially compares each element in the first list to the corresponding element in the second list. The match is true if every element of the first list matches the corresponding element in the second list. The following match is true, because the two lists are identical:

```
( "Zaphod", "Ford", "Trillian" ) ~~ ( "Zaphod", "Ford", "Trillian" )
```

The two lists don't have to be identical, as long as they're the same length and their corresponding elements match:

```
( $zaphod, $ford, $trillian ) ~~ ( "Zaphod", /Ford/, /^T/ )
```

The list-to-list match is also short-circuiting. It stops after the first failed match. This has the same truth value as a series of single-element smart matches linked by and:

```
($zaphod ~~ "Zaphod") and ($ford ~~ /Ford/) and ($trillian ~~ /^T/)
```

Matching arrays

A nonnumeric expression matched against an array sequentially searches for that value in the array. The match is true if the value is found. If @array contains the values "Zaphod", "Ford", and "Trillian", the following match is true when $value is the same as any of those three strings:

```
$value ~~ @array
```

An integer value matched against an array tests the truth of the value at that numeric index. The following match is true if the element @array[2] exists and has a true value:

```
2 ~~ @array
```

An integer value matched against an array reference also does an index lookup:

```
2 ~~ [ "Zaphod", "Ford", "Trillian" ]
```

This match is true, because the third element of the array reference is a true value.

An array matches just like a list of scalar values if it's flattened with the *
operator.* So, the following example searches the array for an element with
the value 2, instead of doing a index lookup:

```
2 ~~ *@array
```

An array matched against a rule does a pattern match across the array. The
match is true if any element of the array matches the rule. If "Trillian", "Gil-
lian", or "million" is an element of @array, the following match is true, no
matter what the other elements are:

```
@array = ( "Zaphod", "Ford", "Trillian" );
@array ~~ /illi/
```

A match of an array against an array sequentially compares each element in
the first array to the corresponding element in the second array:

```
@humans ~~ @vogons
```

This match is true if the two arrays are the same length and @humans[0]
matches @vogons[0], @humans[1] matches @vogons[1], etc.

Matching hashes

A hash matched against any scalar value tests the truth value of the hash
entry with that key:

```
$key ~~ %hash
```

This match is true if the element %hash{$key} exists and has a true value.

A hash matched against a rule does a pattern match on the hash keys:

```
%hash ~~ /bl/
```

This match is true if at least one key in %hash matches "bl".

A hash matched against a hash checks for intersection between the keys of
the two hashes:

```
%vogons ~~ %humans
```

So, this match is true if at least one key from %vogons is also a key of %humans.
If you want to see that two hashes have exactly the same keys, match their
lists of keys:

```
%vogons.keys ~~ %humans.keys
```

A hash matched against an array checks a slice of a hash to see if its values
are true. The match is true if any element of the array is a key in the hash
and the hash value for that key is true:

```
%hash ~~ @array
```

* See "Referencing (or Not)" later in the chapter.

If @array has one element 'blue' and %hash has a corresponding key 'blue', the match is true if %hash{'blue'} has a true value, but false if %hash{'blue'} has a false value ('0', an empty string or undef).

Matching junctions

An expression matched against an any junction is a recursive disjunction. The match is true if at least one of the elements of the list would match in a simple expression-to-expression match:

```
$value ~~ any("Zaphod", "Ford", "Trillian")
```

This example matches if $value is the same as any of the three strings on the right. The effect of this comparison is the same as a simple comparison to a list, except that it isn't guaranteed to compare in any particular order.

A smart match of an all junction is only true when the expression matches every value in the junction:

```
/illi/ ~~ all("Gillian", "million", "Trillian")  # match succeeds
/illi/ ~~ all("Zaphod", "Ford", "Trillian")      # match fails
```

A smart match of a one junction is only true when the expression matches exactly one value in the junction:

```
/illi/ ~~ one("Zaphod", "Ford", "Trillian")      # match succeeds
/illi/ ~~ one("Gillian", "million", "Trillian")  # match fails
```

A smart match of a none junction is true when it doesn't match any values in the junction:

```
/illi/ ~~ none("Zaphod", "Ford", "Marvin")    # match succeeds
/illi/ ~~ none("Zaphod", "Ford", "Trillian")  # match fails
```

An any junction matched against another any junction is a recursive disjunction of every value in the first junction to every value in the second junction. The match is true if at least one value of the first junction matches at least one value in the second junction:

```
any("Ford", "Trillian") ~~ any("Trillian", "Arthur")
```

This match is true, because "Trillian" is in both junctions.

Matching objects

An object matched against a class name is true if the object belongs to that class, or inherits from that class. It's essentially the same as calling the .isa method on the object:

```
$ship ~~ Vogon::Constructor  # $ship.isa(Vogon::Constructor)
```

An object calls a method it's matched against. The match is true if the method returns a true value:

```
$ship ~~ .engage  # $ship.engage
```

Matching subroutines

Any expression matched against a subroutine tests the return value of the subroutine. If the subroutine takes no arguments it is treated as a simple boolean:

```
$value ~~ my_true
```

If the subroutine has a one argument signature and it is the same variable type as the expression, the subroutine is called with the expression as its argument. The return value of the subroutine determines the truth of the match:

```
$value ~~ value_test   # value_test($value)
@array ~~ array_test   # array_test(@array)
%hash ~~ hash_test     # hash_test(%hash)
```

Referencing (or Not)

The unary \ operator returns a reference to its operand. The referencing operator isn't needed very often, since scalar context automatically generates references to arrays, hashes, and functions, but it is still needed in flattening contexts and other contexts that don't auto-reference:

```
@array_of_refs = ( \@a, \@b, \@c );
```

The unary * operator (that's the "splat" operator) flattens a list in a context where it would usually be taken as a reference. On an rvalue, * causes the array to be treated as a simple list:

```
@combo = ( \@array, \%hash);
@a := @combo; # @a is @combo
(@b, %c) := *@combo; # @b is @array, %c is %hash
```

Since the @combo array contains an arrayref and a hashref, an ordinary binding assignment of @combo to @a treats @combo as a single element and binds it to @a. With the flattening operator, the @combo array is treated as a simple list, so each of its elements are bound to a separate element on the left-hand side. @b is bound to the original @array and %c is bound to the original %hash.

On an lvalue, * tells the array to "slurp" all available arguments. An ordinary binding of two arrays to two arrays simply binds the first element on the right-hand side to the first element on the left-hand side, and the second to the second:

```
(@a, @b) := (@c, @d); # @a is @c, @b is @d
*@a := (@c, @d); # @a contains @c and @d
```

So, @a is bound to @c, and @b is bound to @d. With the * operator, the first element on the left-hand side sucks up all the elements on the right-hand side, so @a contains all the elements from @c and @d.

One common use for * is in defining subroutine and method signatures, as you will see in "Subroutines" later in this chapter.

Zip Operator

The ¦ operator takes two lists (arrays, hash keys, etc.) and returns a single list with alternating elements from each of the original lists. This allows loops and other iterative structures to iterate through the elements of several lists at the same time:

```
@a = (1, 2, 3);
@b = (4, 5, 6);

@c = @a ¦ @b; # @c is (1, 4, 2, 5, 3, 6)
```

There is no equivalent ASCII operator for the zip operator, but the zip function is much more fully featured than the operator. It is described in "The for loop" later in this chapter.

Control Structures

The simplest flow of control is linear—one statement follows the next in a straight line to the end of the program. Since this is far too limiting for most situations, languages provide ways to alter the control flow.

Selection

Selection executes one set of actions out of many possible sets. The selection control structures are if, unless, and given.

The if statement

The if statement checks a condition and executes its associated block only if that condition is true. The condition can be any expression that evaluates to a truth value. Parentheses around the condition are optional:

```
if $blue {
    print "True Blue.";
}
```

The if statement can also have an unlimited number of elsif statements that check additional conditions when the preceding conditions are false. The final else statement executes if all preceding if and elsif conditions are false:

```
if $blue {
    print "True Blue.";
} elsif $green {
    print "Green, green, green they say...";
} else {
    print "Colorless green ideas sleep furiously.";
}
```

The unless statement

The unless statement is the logical opposite of if. Its block executes only when the tested condition is false:

```
unless $fire {
    print "All's well.";
}
```

There is no elsunless statement, though else works with unless.

The switch statement

The switch statement selects an action by comparing a given expression, the switch, to a series of when statements, the cases. When a case matches the switch, its block is executed:

```
given $bugblatter {
    when Beast::Trall { close_eyes(); }
    when 'ravenous'   { toss('steak'); }
    when .feeding     { sneak_past(); }
    when /grrr+/      { cover_ears(); }
    when 2            { run_between(); }
    when (3..10)      { run_away(); }

}
```

If these comparisons are starting to look familiar, they should. The set of possible relationships between a given and a when are exactly the same as the left and right side of a smart match operator (~~). The given aliases its argument to $_.* The when is a defaulting construct that does an implicit smart match on $_. The result is the same as if you typed:

```
given $bugblatter {
    when $_ ~~ Beast::Trall { close_eyes(); }
    when $_ ~~ 'ravenous'   { toss('steak'); }
    when $_ ~~ .feeding     { sneak_past(); }
    when $_ ~~ /grrr+/      { cover_ears(); }
    when $_ ~~ 2            { run_between(); }
    when $_ ~~ (3..10)      { run_away(); }
}
```

but much more convenient. In general, only one case is ever executed. Each when statement has an implicit break at the end. It is possible to fall through a case and continue comparing, but since falling through is less common, it is explicitly specified with a continue:

```
given $bugblatter {
    when Beast::Trall { close_eyes(); continue; }
```

---

* $_ is always the current topic (think "topic of conversation"), so the process of aliasing a variable to $_ is known as "topicalization."

```
    when 'ravenous'   { toss('steak'); continue; }
    when 'attacking'  { hurl($spear, $bugblatter); continue; }
    when 'retreating' { toss('towel'); }
}
```

The default case executes its block when all other cases fail:

```
given $bugblatter {
    when Beast::Trall { close_eyes(); }
    when 'ravenous'   { toss('steak'); }
    default { run('away'); }
}
```

Any code within a given will execute, but a successful when skips all remaining code within the given, not just the when statements. This means the default case isn't really necessary, because any code after the final when just acts like a default. But an explicit default case makes the intention of the code clearer in the pure switch. There's more than one way to do it (TMTOWTDI).

```
given $bugblatter {
    print "Slowly I turn...";
    when Beast::Trall { close_eyes(); }
    print "Step by step...";
    when 'ravenous'   { toss('steak'); }
    print "Inch by inch...";
}
```

The when statement can also appear outside a given. When they do, they simply smart match against $_. when statements also have a statement modifier form. It doesn't have an implicit break:

```
print "Zaphod" when 'two heads';
```

Iteration

Iteration executes one set of actions multiple times. Perl 6's loop constructs are while, until, loop, and for.

The while loop

The while loop iterates as long as a condition is true. The condition may be complex, but the result is always a single boolean value because while imposes boolean context on its condition:

```
while $improbability > 1 {
    print "$improbability to 1 against and falling.";
    $improbability = drive_status('power_down');
}
```

until is like while but continues looping as long as the condition is false.

The simple loop

In its simplest form, the loop construct is infinite. It will iterate until a statement within the loop explicitly terminates it:

```
loop {
    print "One more of that Ol' Janx.";
    last if enough( );
}
```

loop is also the counter iterator. Like while, it tests a condition before executing its block each time, but it has added expression slots for initialization and execution between iterations that make it ideal for counter loops:

```
loop ( $counter = 1; $counter < 20; $counter++ ) {
    print "Try to count electric sheep...";
}
```

The for loop

The for loop is the list iterator, so it imposes list context. It takes any list or array, or any expression that produces a list, and loops through the list's elements one at a time. On each iteration, for aliases $_ to the current loop element.* This means all the constructs that default to $_, like print and when, can default to the loop variable:

```
for @useful_things {
    print;
    print " You're one hoopy frood." when 'towel';
}
```

The arrow operator, ->, makes a named alias to the current element, in addition to the $_ alias. All aliases are lexically scoped to the block:

```
for %people.keys -> $name {
    print; # prints $_ (same as $name)
    print ":", %people{$name}{'age'};
}
```

The arrow operator also makes it possible to iterate over multiple loop elements at the same time:

```
for %ages.kv -> $name, $age {
    print $name, " is now ", $age;
}
```

You can combine the arrow operator with the zip function or zip operator to loop over several lists, taking some specified number of elements from each on every iteration, as in the following code.

---

* Topicalization again.

```
# one from each array
for zip(@people,@places,@things) -> $person, $place, $thing {
    print "Are you a $person, $place, or $thing?";
}

# two from each array
for zip(@animals, @things, by=>2)
        -> $animal1, $animal2, $thing1, $thing2 {

    print "The animals, they came, they came in by twosies, twosies: ";
    print "$animal1 and $animal2";

    print "Two things. And I call them, $thing1 and $thing2.";

}

# two from the first array and one from the second
for zip(@colors=>2, @textures=>1) -> $color1, $color2, $texture {
    $mix = blend($color1, $color2);
    draw_circle($mix, $texture);
}
```

Breaking out of loops

The next and last keywords allow you to interrupt the control flow of a
loop. next skips the remaining code in the loop and starts the next iteration.
last skips the remaining code in the loop and terminates the loop:

```
for @useful_things -> $item {
    next when 'towel';
    last when 'bomb';
    print "Are you sure you need your $item?";
}
```

Blocks

In Perl 6, every block is a closure, so you get consistent behavior throughout
the language, whether the block is a control structure, an argument passed
to a subroutine, an anonymous subref, or the definition of a named element
such as a subroutine, method, or class. What is a closure? Closures are
chunks of code that are tied to the lexical scope in which they're defined.
When they're stored and later executed at some point far removed from
their definition, they execute using the variables in their original scope, even
if those variables are no longer accessible any other way. It's almost as if
they package up their lexical scope to make it portable.

The fact that all blocks are closures has some implications. Every block can
have arguments passed to it. This is how for creates a $_ alias for the itera-
tor variable. Every block defines a lexical scope. Every block has the potential to be stored and executed later. Whether a block is stored or executed

immediately depends on the structure that uses it. The control structures we've discussed so far all execute their blocks where they're defined. A bare block executes immediately when it's alone, but is stored when it's in an assignment context or passed as a parameter:

```
# executed immediately
{
    print "Zaphod";
}

# stored
$closure = {
    print "Trillian";
}
```

my, our, temp, and let

my and our are different ways of declaring variables. my declares a variable in the current lexical scratchpad, while our declares a lexical alias to a variable in the package symbol table.

```
my $lexical_var;
our $package_var;
```

temp and let are not declarations, they are runtime commands to store off the current value of a variable so it can be restored later. temp variables always restore their previous value on exiting the lexical scope of the temp, while let variables keep the temporary value, unless they are explicitly told to restore it:

```
temp $throwaway;
let $hypothetical;
```

Property blocks

Every block may have a series of control flow handlers attached to it. These are called "property blocks" because they are themselves blocks (i.e., closures), attached as properties on the block. Property blocks are defined within their enclosing block by an uppercase keyword followed by a block (they're also sometimes called NAMED blocks):

```
NEXT {
    print "Coming around again."
}
```

Property blocks aren't executed in sequential order with the other code in the enclosing block—they are stored at compile time and executed at the appropriate point in the control flow. NEXT executes between each iteration of a loop, LAST executes at the end of the final iteration (or simply at the end of an ordinary block). PRE and POST are intended for assertion checking and cannot have any side effects. PRE executes before everything else in the block, and POST executes after everything else in the loop. CATCH, KEEP, and UNDO are related to exception handling. KEEP and UNDO are variants of LAST and execute after CATCH. KEEP executes when the block exits with no exceptions, or when all exceptions have been trapped and handled; UNDO executes when the block exits with untrapped exceptions.

This example prints out its loop variable in the body of the block:

```
for 1..4 {
    NEXT { print " potato, "; }
    LAST { print "." }
    print;

}
```

Between each iteration, the NEXT block executes, printing "potato". At the end of the final iteration, the LAST block prints a period. So the final result is "1 potato, 2 potato, 3 potato, 4".

Property blocks are lexically scoped within their enclosing block, so they have access to lexical variables defined there.

```
for 5..7 -> $count {
    my $potato = " potato, ";
    NEXT {
        print $count, $potato;
    }
    LAST {
        print $count, $potato, "more.";
    }
}
```

Exceptions

There are two types of exceptions: error exceptions and control flow exceptions. All exceptions are stored in the error object $!. Exceptions are classes that inherit from the Exception class.

Error exceptions are thrown by throw, die, and fail (under use fatal). Any block can be an error exception handler. All it needs is a CATCH block. CATCH blocks always topicalize $!, so the simplest way to test for a particular exception is to compare it to a class name using a when statement.[*]

```
CATCH {
    when Err::Danger { warn "fly away home"; }
}
```

---

[*] See the earlier section "Smart Match" for a complete set of comparison relations.

The $! object will also stringify to its text message if you match it against a pattern.

```
CATCH {
    when /:w I'm sorry Dave/ { warn "HAL is in the house."; }
}
```

If the CATCH block is exited by an explicit break statement, or by an implicit break in a when or default case, it marks the exception as clean. Otherwise, it rethrows the exception to be caught by some outer block.

Once an exception is thrown, execution skips straight to the CATCH block and the remaining code in the block is skipped. If the block has POST, KEEP, or UNDO property blocks, they will execute after the CATCH block.

Control flow exceptions handle alterations in the flow of control that aren't errors. When you call next to skip the remaining code in the loop and go on to the next iteration, you're actually throwing a control exception. These exceptions are caught by the relevant control structure: next and last exceptions are caught by loops, a return exception is caught by a subroutine or method, etc.

Subroutines

The most basic form of a subroutine is simply the sub keyword, followed by the name of the sub, followed by the block that defines the sub:

```
sub alert {
    print "We have normality.";
}
```

In a simple sub, all arguments are passed in the @_ array:

```
sub sum {
    my $sum;
    for @_ -> $number {
        $sum += $number;
    }
    return $sum;
}
```

Formal Parameters

Perl 6 subroutines can define named formal parameters. The parameter list is part of the subroutine definition, often called the "signature" of the subroutine:

```
sub standardize ($text, $method) {
    my $clean;
    given $method {
```

```
            when 'length' { $clean = wrap($text, 72); }
            when 'lower'  { $clean = lowercase($text); }
            ...
        }
        return $clean;
    }
```

Subroutine parameter lists are non-flattening. Any array or hash passed into a subroutine is treated as a single parameter. An array in the signature expects to be passed an actual array or arrayref, and a hash expects a hash or hashref:

```
    sub whole (@names, %flags) {
        ...
    }

    # and elsewhere
    whole(@array, %hash);
```

To get the old-style behavior where the elements of an array (or the pairs of a hash) flatten out into the parameter list, use the flattening operator in the call to the subroutine. Here, $first is bound to @array[0] and $second is bound to @array[1]:

```
    sub flat ($first, $second) {
        ...
    }

    flat(*@array);
```

To make an array (or hash) in the parameter list slurp up all the arguments passed to it, use the flattening operator in the signature definition. These are known as variadic parameters because they can take a variable number of arguments. Here, @names[0] is bound to $zaphod, and @names[1] to $ford:

```
    sub slurp (*@names) {
        ...
    }

    slurp($zaphod, $ford);
```

Subroutines with defined parameter lists don't get an @_ array. In fact, a simple subroutine without a signature actually has an implicit signature of *@_:

```
    sub simple {
        ...
    }
    # is the same as
    sub simple (*@_) {
        ...
    }
```

By default, parameters are passed by reference, but marked as constant so they cannot be modified within the body of the subroutine. The is rw property marks a parameter as modifiable, so changes to the parameter within the body of the sub modify the original variable passed in. The is copy property marks a parameter as passed by value, so the parameter is a lexically scoped copy of the original value passed in:

```
sub passbyvalue ($first is copy, $second is copy) {
    ...
}

sub modifyparams ($first is rw, $second is rw) {
    ...
}
```

Optional parameters are marked with a ? before the parameter name:

```
sub someopt ($required1, $required2, ?$optional1, ?$optional2) {
    ...
}
```

A parameter can define the type of argument that will be passed to it. The type is defined before the argument name:

```
sub typedparams ( Int $first, Str $second) {
    ...
}
```

Named parameter passing

The standard way of passing parameters is by position. The first argument passed in goes to the first parameter, the second to the second, and so on:

```
sub matchparams ($first, $second) {
    ...
}

matchparams($one, $two);   # $one is bound to $first
                           # $two is bound to $second
```

You can also pass parameters in by name, using a list of anonymous pairs. The key of each pair gives the parameter's name and the value of the pair gives the value to be bound to the parameter. When passed by name, the arguments can come in any order. Optional parameters can be left out, even if they come in the middle of the parameter list. This is particularly useful for subroutines with a large number of optional parameters:

```
sub namedparams ($first, ?$second, ?$third is rw) {
    ...
}

namedparams(third => 'Trillian', first => $name);
```

You can specify that certain parameters will be passed only by name, never by position, with a + in place of the ? to mark optional parameters:

```
sub namedparams ($first, +$second, +$third is rw) {
    ...
}
```

Multimethods

You can define multiple routines with the same name but different signatures. These are known as "multimethods" and defined with the multi keyword instead of sub. They're useful if you want a routine that can handle different types of arguments in different ways, but still appear as a single subroutine to the user. For example, you might define an add multimethod with different behavior for integers, floats, and certain types of numeric objects:

```
multi add (Int $first, Int $second) { ... }
multi add (Num $first, Num $second) { ... }
multi add (Imaginary $first, Imaginary $second) { ... }
multi add (MyNum $first, MyNum $second) { ... }
```

When you later call the routine:

```
add($count, $total);
```

it will dispatch to the right version of add based on the types of the arguments passed to it.

Lexical Scope

Subroutines can be lexically scoped just like variables. A my-ed subroutine makes an entry in the current lexical scratchpad with a & sigil. They're called just like a normal subroutine:

```
if $dining {
    my sub dine ($who, $where) {
        ...
    }

    dine($zaphod, "Milliways");
}

dine($arthur, "Nutri-Matic");  # error
```

The first call to the lexically scoped dine is fine, but the second is a compile-time error because dine doesn't exist in the outer scope.

Anonymous Subroutines

Anonymous subroutines do everything that ordinary subroutines do. They can define a formal parameter list with optional and required parameters, take positional and named arguments, and do variadic slurping. The only difference is that they don't define a name. They have to get the equivalent of a name somewhere, whether they're assigned to a variable, passed as a parameter, aliased to another subroutine, or some other way. You can't call a subroutine if you have no way to refer to it:

```
$make_tea = sub ($tealeaves, ?$sugar, ?$milk) { ... }
```

The arrow operator used with for and given is just another way of defining anonymous subroutines. The arrow doesn't require parentheses around its parameter list, but it can't separate required and optional parameters and can't be used to define named subs:

```
$make_tea = -> $tealeaves, $sugar, $milk { ... }
```

A bare block can also define an anonymous subroutine, but it can't define a formal parameter list on the sub and can't define a named sub.

```
$make_tea = {
    my $tea = boil 'tealeaves';
    combine $tea, 'sugar', 'milk';
    return $tea;
}
```

Placeholder Variables

Placeholder variables provide the advantages of automatically named parameters, without the inconvenience of defining a formal parameter list. You just use variables with a caret after the sigil—$^name, @^name, or %^name—within the subroutine's block, and the arguments passed into the subroutine are bound to them. The order of the parameters is determined by the Unicode sorting order of the placeholder's names, so the example below acts as if it has a formal parameter list of ($^milk, $^sugar, $^tealeaves):

```
$make_tea = {
    my $tea = boil $^tealeaves;
    combine $tea, $^sugar, $^milk;
    return $tea;
}
```

They're handy in short subroutines and bare blocks, but get unwieldy quickly in anything more complicated:

```
@sorted = sort { $^a <=> $^b } @array;
```

Currying

Currying allows you to create a shortcut for calling a subroutine with some preset parameter values. The assuming method takes a list of named arguments and returns a subroutine reference, with each of the named arguments bound to the original subroutine's parameter list:

```
sub multiply ($multiplicand, $multiplier) {
    return $multiplicand * $multiplier;
}

$six_times = &multiply.assuming(multiplier => 6);

$six_times(9); # 54
$six_times(7); # 42
...
```

If you have a subroutine multiply that multiplies two numbers, you might create a subref $six_times that sets the value for the $multiplier parameter, so you can reuse it several times.

Classes and Objects

Class syntax won't really be decided until Apocalypse 12, so this section is the most sketchy and likely to change of any in the chapter. Rather than roll out a lengthy speculation, we focus on the parts that are relatively certain.

Class declarations have two forms. The most basic is a class declaration statement, followed by the code that defines the class. There can be only one class or module declaration statement in a file. All code that follows is defined in the Heart::Gold namespace:

```
class Heart::Gold;
# class definition follows
...
```

The other form wraps the declaration and definition into a block. Everything within the class's block is defined in the namespace of the class. You can have as many of these as you like in a file, and embed one class within the block of another:

```
class Heart::Gold {
    # class definition enclosed
    ...
}
```

To create a new object from a class, simply call its new method. A default new method is provided in the universal base class Object:

```
$ship = Heart::Gold.new(length => 150);
```

Attributes

Attributes are the data at the core of a class. They are commonly known as instance variables, data members, or instance attributes. They're declared with the has keyword, and always have a "." after the sigil:

```
class Heart::Gold {
    has $.height;
    has $.length;
    has @.cargo;
    has %.crew;
    ...
}
```

Attributes also automatically generate their own accessor method with the same name as the attribute:

```
$obj.height( ) # returns the value of $.height
```

By default, all attributes and their accessor methods are private to the class. If you want them to be accessible from outside the class, flag them with the is public trait:

```
has $.height is public;
```

Methods

Methods are similar to subroutines, but different enough to merit their own keyword, method. The most obvious differences are that they're always invoked on an object (or class), and they always pass their invocant (that is, the object or class on which they were invoked) as an implicit argument. The invocant is marked off from the other parameters in the list by a colon, as follows:

```
method initiate_drive ($self: $power, $tea) {
    ...
}
```

Methods topicalize their invocant, so it's always accessible as $_, even if the method doesn't include it in the parameter list or has no parameter list. This is particularly handy since any method called without an explicit object defaults to $_:

```
method shut_down (: $drive){
    if .safe {
        .powerdown($drive);
    }
    return .status;
}
```

Methods are public by default, but can be made private to the class with the is private trait:

```
method inaccessible is private ($self: $value) {
    ...
}
```

Inheritance

Any class can inherit methods from another class using the is keyword* in the class declaration. Both public and private methods are inherited by the derived class, but only public methods are directly accessible in the derived class:

```
use Ship;
class Heart::Gold is Ship {
    ....
}
```

Inherited attributes are only accessible within the derived class through their accessor methods:

```
class Ship {
    has $.height;
    has $.length;
    ...
}

class Heart::Gold is Ship {
    method dimensions ($self:){
        print "$self.length  x $self.height \n";
    }
}
```

Lexically Scoped Classes

Classes in Perl 6 are first class entities with entries in the symbol table.† This means classes can be lexically scoped, just like variables or subroutines:

```
my class Infinite::Improbablity {
    ...
}

$drive = Infinite::Improbability.new( );
```

---

* This is the same keyword as compile-time properties. The fact that a class inherits from some other class is really just a trait of the inheriting class.

† If you're curious, their sigil is ::, though it's never needed in code.

A my-ed class works just like any other class, but is accessible only within the lexical scope where it's defined.

Anonymous Classes

You can also define anonymous classes and create objects from them:

```
$class = class {
    ...
}

$object = $class.new( );
```

A class's block is a closure, just like every other block, so it has access to variables from its defining scope, no matter where it's actually used.

Subroutines in Classes

You can also define ordinary subroutines within a class. They cannot be invoked on an object with the $object.methodname syntax, will never pass an implicit invocant argument, and aren't inherited. They're mainly useful for utility code internal to the class:

```
class Answer::Young;

has $.answer;
...
sub is_valid ($value) {
    return 1 if 10 < $value < 42;
}
...
method set_answer (: $new) {
    $.answer = $new if is_valid($new);
}
```

Grammars and Rules

Perl 6 "regular expressions" are so far beyond the formal definition of regular expressions that we decided it was time for a more meaningful name.* We now call them "rules." Perl 6 rules bring the full power of recursive descent parsing to the core of Perl, but are comfortably useful even if you don't know anything about recursive descent parsing. A grammar is a collection of rules, in the same way that a class is a collection of methods.

---

* Regular expressions describe regular languages, and consist of three primitives and a limited set of operations (three or so, depending on the formulation). So, even Perl 5 "regular expressions" weren't formal regular expressions.

Basic Rule Syntax

A rule is just a pattern for matching text. Rules can match right where they're defined, or they can be stored up to match later. Rules can be named or anonymous. They may be defined with variations on the familiar /.../ syntax, or using subroutine-like syntax with the keyword rule. Table 4-2 shows the basic syntax for defining rules.

Table 4-2. Rules

Syntax	Meaning
m/.../	Match a pattern (immediate execution).
s/.../.../	Perform a substitution (immediate execution).
rx/.../	Define an anonymous rule (deferred execution).
/.../	Immediately match or define an anonymous rule, depending on the context.
rule { ... }	Define an anonymous rule.
rule name { ... }	Define a named rule.

?...? and (...) are no longer valid replacements for the /.../ delimiters, but you can use other standard quoting characters as replacement delimiters. The unary context forcing operators, +, ?, and ~, interact with the bare /.../. +/.../ immediately matches and returns a count of matches. ?/.../ immediately matches and returns a boolean value of success or failure. ~/.../ immediately matches and returns the matched string value. The results are the ordinary behavior of /.../ in numeric, boolean, and string contexts. The bare /.../ also matches immediately in void context, or when it's an argument of the smart match operator (~~). In all other contexts, it constructs an anonymous rule.

Building Blocks

Every pattern is built out of a series of metacharacters, metasymbols, bracketing symbols, escape sequences, and assertions of various types. These are the basic vocabulary of pattern matching. The most basic set of metacharacters is shown in Table 4-3.

Table 4-3. Metacharacters

Symbol	Meaning
.	Match any single character, including a newline.
^	Match the beginning of a string.
$	Match the end of a string.

Table 4-3. Metacharacters (continued)

Symbol	Meaning
^^	Match the beginning of a line.
$$	Match the end of a line.
|	Separate alternate patterns.
\	Escape a metacharacter to get a literal character, or escape a literal character to get a metacharacter.
#	Mark a comment (to the end of the line).
:=	Bind the result of a match to a hypothetical variable.
(...)	Group patterns and capture the result.
[...]	Group patterns without capturing.
{...}	Execute a closure (Perl 6 code) within a rule.
<...>	Assertion delimiters.

By default, rules ignore literal whitespace within the pattern. You can put the # comment marker at the end of any line. Just make sure you don't comment out the symbol that terminates the rule. Closures within bare {...} are always a successful zero-width match, unless they explicitly call the fail function. Assertions, marked with <...> delimiters, handle a variety of constructs, including character classes and user-defined quantifiers. The built-in quantifiers are shown in Table 4-4.

Table 4-4. Quantifiers

Maximal	Minimal	Meaning
*	*?	Match 0 or more times.
+	+?	Match 1 or more times.
?	??	Match 0 or 1 times.
<n>	<n>?	Match exactly *n* times.
<n..m>	<n..m>?	Match at least *n* and no more than *m* times.
<n...>	<n...>?	Match at least *n* times.

n..m is the range quantifier, so it uses the range operator "..". *n...* is shorthand for *n..*Inf and matches as many times as possible.

Table 4-5 shows the escape sequences for special characters. With all the escape sequences that use brackets, (...), {...}, and <...> work in place of [...]. An ordinary variable now interpolates as a literal string, so \Q is rarely needed.

Table 4-5. Escape sequences

Escape	Meaning
\o[...]	Match a character given in octal (brackets optional).
\b	Match a word boundary.
\B	Match when not on a word boundary.
\c[...]	Match a named character or control character.
\C[...]	Match any character except the bracketed named or control character.
\d	Match a digit.
\D	Match a non-digit.
\e	Match an escape character.
\E	Match anything but an escape character.
\f	Match the form feed character.
\F	Match anything but a form feed.
\n	Match a newline.
\N	Match anything but a newline.
\h	Match horizontal whitespace.
\H	Match anything but horizontal whitespace.
\L[...]	Everything within the brackets is lowercase.
\r	Match a return.
\R	Match anything but a return.
\s	Match any whitespace character.
\S	Match anything but whitespace.
\t	Match a tab.
\T	Match anything but a tab.
\U[...]	Everything within the brackets is uppercase.
\v	Match vertical whitespace.
\V	Match anything but vertical whitespace.
\w	Match a word character (Unicode alphanumeric plus "_").
\W	Match anything but a word character.
\x[...]	Match a character given in hexadecimal (brackets optional).
\X[...]	Match anything but the character given in hexadecimal (brackets optional).
\Q[...]	All metacharacters within the brackets match as literal characters.

Modifiers

Modifiers alter the meaning of the pattern syntax. The standard position for modifiers is at the beginning of the rule, right after the m, s, or rx, or after the

name in a named rule. Modifiers cannot attach to the outside of a bare /.../.
For example:

```
m:i/marvin/ # case insensitive
rule names :i { marvin | ford | arthur }
```

The single-character modifiers can be grouped, but the others must be separated by a colon:

```
m:iwe/ zaphod / # Ok
m:ignorecase:words:each/ zaphod / # Ok
m:ignorecasewordseach / zaphod / # Not Ok
```

Most of the modifiers can also go inside the rule, attached to the rule delimiters or to grouping delimiters. Internal modifiers are lexically scoped to their enclosing delimiters, so you get a temporary alteration of the pattern:

```
m/:w I saw [:i zaphod] / # only 'zaphod' is case insensitive
```

Really, it's only the repetition modifiers that can't be lexically scoped, because they alter the return value of the entire rule. Table 4-6 shows the current list of modifiers.

Table 4-6. Modifiers

Short	Long	Meaning
:i	:ignorecase	Case-insensitive match.
:I		Case-sensitive match (on by default).
:c	:cont	Continue where the previous match on the string left off.
:w	:words	Literal whitespace in the pattern matches as \s+ or \s*.
:W		Turn off intelligent whitespace matching (return to default).
	:Nx/:x(N)	Match the pattern N times.
	:Nth/:nth(N)	Match the Nth occurrence of a pattern.
	:once	Match the pattern only once.
:e	:each	Match the pattern as many times as possible, but only possibilities that don't overlap.
	:any	Match every possible occurrence of a pattern, even overlapping possibilities.
	:u0	. is a byte.
	:u1	. is a Unicode codepoint.
	:u2	. is a Unicode grapheme.
	:u3	. is language dependent.
	:p5	The pattern uses Perl 5 regex syntax.

:w makes patterns sensitive to literal whitespace, but in an intelligent way. Any cluster of literal whitespace acts like an explicit \s+ when it separates two identifiers and \s* everywhere else.

The :Nth modifier also has the alternate forms :Nst, :Nnd, and :Nrd for cases where it's more natural to write :1st, :2nd, :3rd than it is to write :1th, :2th, :3th. Either way is valid, so pick the one that's most comfortable for you.

There are no modifiers to alter whether the matched string is treated as a single line or multiple lines. That's why the "beginning of string" and "end of string" metasymbols now have "beginning of line" and "end of line" counterparts.

Assertions

Assertions hold many different constructs with many different purposes. In general, an assertion simply states that some condition or state is true and the match fails when that assertion is false. Table 4-7 shows the syntax for assertions.

Table 4-7. Assertions

Syntax	Meaning
<...>	Generic assertion delimiter.
<name>	Match a named rule or character class.
<!...>	Negate any assertion.
<[...]>	Match an enumerated character class.
<-...>	Complement a character class (named or enumerated).
<"...">	Match a literal string (interpolated at match time).
<'...'>	Match a literal string (not interpolated).
<(...)>	Boolean assertion. Execute a closure and match if it returns a true result.
<$scalar>	Match an anonymous rule.
<@array>	Match a series of anonymous rules as alternates.
<%hash>	Match a key from the hash, then its value (which is an anonymous rule).
<&sub( )>	Match an anonymous rule returned by a sub.
<{ code }>	Match an anonymous rule returned by a closure.
<.>	Match any logical grapheme, including combining character sequences.

<(...)> is similar to {...}, in that it allows you to include straight Perl code within a rule. The difference is that <(...)> evaluates the return value of the closure in boolean context. The match succeeds if the return is true and fails if the return is false.

A bare scalar within a pattern interpolates as a literal string, an array matches as a series of alternate literal strings, and by default a hash matches a word (\w+) and tries to find that word as one of its keys.* You have to enclose a variable in assertion delimiters to get it to interpolate as an anonymous rule or rules.†

Built-in Rules

A number of named rules are provided by default, including a complete set of POSIX-style classes, and Unicode property classes. The list isn't fully defined yet, but Table 4-8 shows a few you're likely to see.

Table 4-8. Built-in rules

Rule	Meaning
`<alpha>`	Match a Unicode alphabetic character.
`<digit>`	Match a digit.
`<sp>`	Match a single space character (the same as \s).
`<ws>`	Match any whitespace (the same as \s+).
`<null>`	Match the null string.
`<prior>`	Match the same thing as the previous match.
`<before ...>`	Lookahead. Assert that you're *before* a pattern.
`<after ...>`	Lookbehind. Assert that you're *after* a pattern.
`<prop ...>`	Match any character with the named property.
`<replace(...)>`	Replace everything matched so far in the rule or subrule with the given string (under consideration).

The null pattern `//` is no longer valid syntax for rules. The built-in rule `<null>` matches a zero-width string (so it's always true) and `<prior>` matches whatever the most recent successful rule matched.

Backtracking Control

Backtracking is triggered whenever part of the pattern fails to match. You can also explicitly trigger backtracking by calling the `fail` function within a closure. Table 4-9 shows some metacharacters and built-in rules relevant to backtracking.

---

* The effect is much as if it matched the keys as a series of alternates, but you're guaranteed to match the longest possible key, instead of just the first one it hits in random order.
† This is the old Perl 5 behavior of a variable interpolating as a regex, but with a kick.

Table 4-9. Backtracking controls

Operator	Meaning
:	Don't retry the previous atom, fail to the next earlier atom.
::	Don't backtrack over this point, fail out of the closest enclosing group ((...), [...], or the rule delimiters).
:::	Don't backtrack over this point, fail out of the current rule or subrule.
<commit>	Don't backtrack over this point, fail out of the entire match (even from within a subrule).
<cut>	Like <commit>, but also cuts the string matched. The point of the <cut> becomes the new beginning of the string.

Hypothetical Variables

Hypothetical variables are a powerful way of building up data structures from within a match. An ordinary capture with (...) stores the result of the capture in $1, $2, etc. The values stored in these variables will be kept if the match is successful, but thrown away if the match fails (hence the term "hypothetical"). The numbered capture variables are accessible outside the match, but only within the immediate surrounding lexical scope:

```
"Zaphod Beeblebrox" ~~ m:w/ (\w+) (\w+) /;

print $1; # prints Zaphod
```

You can also capture into any user-defined variable with the binding operator :=. These variables must already be defined in the lexical scope surrounding the rule:

```
my $person;
"Zaphod's just this guy." ~~ / ^ $person := (\w+) /;
print $person; # prints Zaphod
```

Repeated matches can be captured into an array:

```
my @words;
"feefifofum" ~~ / @words := (f<-[f]>+)* /;
# ("fee", "fi", "fo", "fum")
```

Pairs of repeated matches can be captured into a hash:

```
my %customers;
$records ~~ m:w/ %customers := [ <id> = <name> \n]* /;
```

If you don't need the captured value outside the rule, use a $? variable instead. These are lexically scoped to the rule:

```
"Zaphod saw Zaphod" ~~ m:w/ $?name := (\w+) \w+ $?name/;
```

A match of a named rule stores the result in a $? variable with the same name as the rule. These variables are also accessible only within the rule:

```
"Zaphod saw Zaphod" ~~ m:w/ <name> \w+ $?name /;
```

Grammars

Sometimes you don't want one rule, you need a whole collection of rules, especially for complex text parsing. Rules live in a grammar, like methods live in a class. In fact, grammars are classes, they're just classes that inherit from the universal Rule class. This means that grammars can inherit from other grammars, and that they define a namespace for their rules.

```
grammar Hitchhikers {
    rule name :w {
        Zaphod :: [Beeblebrox]?
        | Ford :: [Prefect]?
        | Arthur :: [Dent]?
    }

    rule id :w { \d<10> }
}
```

Any rule in the current grammar or in one of its parents can be called directly, but rules from other grammars need to have their package specified:

```
if $newsrelease ~~ /<Hitchhiker.name>/ {
    send_alert($1);
}
```

## CHAPTER 5

Parrot Internals

"What is the tortoise standing on?"
"You're very clever, young man,
very clever," said the old lady.
"But it's turtles all the way down!"
—Stephen Hawking
  A Brief History of Time

This chapter details the architecture and internal workings of Parrot, the interpreter behind Perl 6. Parrot is a register-based, bytecode-driven, object-oriented, multithreaded, dynamically typed, self-modifying, asynchronous interpreter. While that's an awful lot of buzzwords, the design fits together remarkably well.

Core Design Principles

Three main principles drive the design of Parrot—speed, abstraction, and stability.

Speed is a paramount concern. Parrot absolutely must be as fast as possible, since the engine effectively imposes an upper limit on the speed of any program running on it. It doesn't matter how efficient your program is or how clever your program's algorithms are if the engine it runs on limps along. While Parrot can't make a poorly written program run fast, it could make a well-written program run slowly, a possibility we find entirely unacceptable.

Speed encompasses more than just raw execution time. It extends to resource usage. It's irrelevant how fast the engine can run through its byte-code if it uses so much memory in the process that the system spends half its time swapping to disk. While we're not averse to using resources to gain speed benefits, we try not to use more than we need, and to share what we do use.

Abstraction indicates that things are designed such that there's a limit to what anyone needs to keep in their head at any one time. This is very important because Parrot is conceptually very large, as you'll see when you read the rest of the chapter. There's a lot going on, too much to keep the whole thing in mind at once. The design is such that you don't have to remember what everything does, and how it all works. This is true regardless of whether you're writing code that runs on top of Parrot or working on one of its internal subsystems.

Parrot also uses abstraction boundaries as places to cheat for speed. As long as it *looks* like an abstraction is being completely fulfilled, it doesn't matter if it actually *is* being fulfilled, something we take advantage of in many places within the engine. For example, variables are required to be able to return a string representation of themselves, and each variable type has a "give me your string representation" function we can call. That lets each class have custom stringification code, optimized for that particular type. The engine has no idea what goes on beneath the covers and doesn't care—it just knows to call that function when it needs the string value of a variable.

Stability is important for a number of reasons. We're building the Parrot engine to be a good backend for many language compilers to target. We must maintain a stable interface so compiled programs can continue to run as time goes by. We're also working hard to make Parrot a good interpreter for embedded languages, so we must have a stable interface exposed to anyone who wants to embed us. Finally, we want to avoid some of the problems that Perl 5 has had over the years that forced C extensions written to be recompiled after an upgrade. Recompiling C extensions is annoying during the upgrade and potentially fraught with danger. Such backward-incompatible changes have sometimes been made to Perl itself.

Parrot's Architecture

The Parrot system is divided into four main parts, each with its own specific task. The diagram in Figure 5-1 shows the parts, and the way source code and control flows through Parrot. Each of the four parts of Parrot are covered briefly here, with the features and parts of the interpreter covered in more detail afterward.

The flow starts with source code, which is passed into the parser module. The parser processes that source into a form that the compiler module can handle. The compiler module takes the processed source and emits bytecode, which Parrot can directly execute. That bytecode is passed into the optimizer module, which processes the bytecode and produces bytecode that is hopefully faster than what the compiler emitted. Finally, the bytecode is

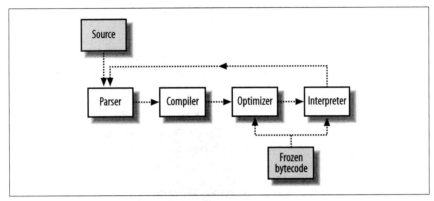

Figure 5-1. Parrot's flow

handed off to the interpreter module, which interprets the bytecode. Since compilation and execution are so tightly woven in Perl, the control may well end up back at the parser to parse more code.

Parrot's compiler module also has the capability to freeze bytecode to disk and read that frozen bytecode back again, bypassing the parser and compilation phases entirely. The bytecode can be directly executed, or handed to the optimizer to work on before execution. This may happen if you've loaded in a precompiled library and want Parrot to optimize the combination of your code and the library code. The bytecode loader is interesting in its own right, and also warrants a small section.

Parser

The parser module is responsible for taking source code in and turning it into an Abstract Syntax Tree (AST). An AST is a digested form of the program, one that's much more amenable to manipulation. In some systems this task is split into two parts—the lexing and the parsing—but since the tasks are so closely bound, Parrot combines them into a single module.

Lexing (or tokenizing) turns a stream of characters into a stream of tokens. It doesn't assign any meaning to those tokens—that's the job of the parser— but it is smart enough to see that $a = 1 + 2; is composed of 6 tokens ($, a, =, 1, +, and 2).

Parsing is the task of taking the tokens that the lexer has found and assigning some meaning to them. Sometimes the parser emits executable code of a sort, when the parsed output can be directly executed.

Parsing can be a chore, as anyone who's done it before knows. In some cases it can be downright maddening—Perl 5's parser has over ten thousand lines of C code. Utility programs such as *lex* and *yacc* are often used to automate the generation of parser code. Perl 5 itself uses a *yacc*-processed grammar to handle some of the task of parsing Perl code.*

Rather than going with a custom-built parser for each language, Parrot provides a general-purpose parser built on top of Perl 6's regular expression engine, with hooks for calling out to special-purpose code where necessary. Perl 6 grammar rules are designed to be powerful enough to handle parsing Perl, so it made good sense to leverage the engine as a general-purpose parser. Parrot provides some utility code to transform a *yacc* grammar into a Perl 6 grammar, so languages that already use *yacc* can be moved over to Parrot's parser with a minimum amount of fuss. This allows you to use a *yacc* grammar instead of a Perl 6 grammar to describe the language being parsed, both because many languages already have their grammars described with *yacc* and because a *yacc* grammar is sometimes a more appropriate way to describe things.

Parrot does support independent parsers for cases where the Perl 6 regex engine isn't the appropriate choice. A language might already have an existing parser available, or different techniques might be in order. The Perl 5 parsing engine may get embedded this way, as it's easier to embed a quirky existing parser than it is to recreate all the quirks in a new parser.

Compiler

The compiler module takes the AST that the parser generates and turns it into code that the interpreter engine can execute. This translation is very straightforward. It involves little more than flattening the AST and running the flattened tree though a series of substitutions.

The compiler is the least interesting part of Parrot. It transforms one machine representation of your program—the AST that the parser generated—into another machine representation of your program—the bytecode that the interpreter needs. It's little more than a simple, rule-based filter module, albeit one that's necessary for Parrot to understand your source code.

Optimizer

The optimizer module takes the AST that the parser generated and the bytecode that the compiler generated, and transforms the bytecode to make it run faster.

---

* *yacc* can handle only part of the task, though. As the quote goes, "The task of parsing Perl is divided between *lex*, *yacc*, smoke, and mirrors."

Optimizing code for dynamic languages such as Perl, Python, and Ruby is an interesting task. The languages are so dynamic that the optimizer can't be sure how a program will actually run. For example, the code:

```
$a = 0;
for (1..10000);
    $a++;
}
```

looks straightforward enough. The variable $a starts at 0, gets incremented ten thousand times, and has an end value of 10000. A standard optimizer would turn that code into the single line:

```
$a = 10000;
```

and remove the loop entirely. Unfortunately, that's not necessarily appropriate for Perl. $a could easily be tied, perhaps representing the position of some external hardware. If incrementing the variable ten thousand times smoothly moves a stepper motor from 0 to 10000 in increments of one, just assigning a value of 10000 to the variable might whip the motor forward in one step, damaging the hardware. A tied variable might also keep track of the number of times it has been accessed or modified. Either way, optimizing the loop away changes the semantics of the program in ways the original programmer didn't want.

Because of the potential for active or tied data, especially for languages as dynamically typed as Perl, optimizing is a non-trivial task. Other languages, such as C or Pascal, are more statically typed and lack active data, so an aggressive optimizer is in order for them. Breaking out the optimizer into a separate module allows us to add in optimizations piecemeal without affecting the compiler. There's a lot of exciting work going into the problem of optimizing dynamic languages, and we fully expect to take advantage of it where we can.

Optimization is potentially an expensive operation, another good reason to have it in a separate module. Spending ten seconds optimizing a program that will run in five seconds is a huge waste of time when using Perl's traditional compile-and-go model—optimizing the code will make the program run slower. On the other hand, spending ten seconds to optimize a program makes sense if you save the optimized version to disk and use it over and over again. Even if you save only one second per program run, it doesn't take long for the ten-second optimization time to pay off. The default is to optimize heavily when freezing bytecode to disk and lightly when running directly, but this can be changed with a command-line switch.

Perl 5, Python, and Ruby all lack a robust optimizer (outside their regular expression engines), so any optimizations we add will increase their performance. This, we feel, is a good thing.

Interpreter

The interpreter module is the part of the engine that executes the generated bytecode. Calling it an interpreter is something of a misnomer, since Parrot's core includes both a traditional bytecode interpreter module as well as a high-performance JIT engine, but you can consider that an implementation detail.

All the interesting things happen inside the interpreter, and the remainder of the chapter is dedicated to the interpreter and the functions it provides. It's not out of line to consider the interpreter as the real core of Parrot, and to consider the parser, compiler, and optimizer as utility modules whose ultimate purpose is to feed bytecode to the interpreter.

Bytecode Loader

The bytecode loader isn't part of our block diagram, but it is interesting enough to warrant brief coverage.

The bytecode loader handles loading in bytecode that's been frozen to disk. The Parrot bytecode loader is clever enough to handle loading in Parrot bytecode regardless of the sort of system that it was saved on, so we have cross-system portability. You can generate bytecode on a 32-bit x86 system and load it up on a 64-bit Alpha or SPARC system without any problems.

The bytecode loading system also has a heuristic engine built into it, so it can identify the bytecode format it's reading. This means Parrot can not only tell what sort of system Parrot bytecode was generated on so it can properly process it, but also allows it to identify bytecode generated for other bytecode driven systems, such as .NET, the JVM, and the Z-machine.

Together with Parrot's loadable opcode library system (something we'll talk about later), this gives Parrot the capability to load in foreign bytecode formats and transform them into something Parrot can execute. With a sophisticated enough loader, Parrot can load and execute Java and .NET bytecode and present Java and .NET library code to languages that generate native Parrot bytecode. This is something of a happy accident. The original purpose of the architecture was to allow Parrot to load and execute Z-machine bytecode,[*] but happy accidents are the best kind.

---

[*] The Z-machine is the interpreter for Infocom text adventures, such as Zork and The Lurking Horror.

The Interpreter

The interpreter is the engine that actually runs the code emitted by the parser, compiler, and optimizer modules. The Parrot execution engine is a virtual CPU done completely in software. We've drawn on research in CPU and interpreter design over the past forty years to try and build the best engine to run dynamic languages.

That emphasis on dynamic languages is important. We are not trying to build the fastest C, Forth, Lisp, or Prolog engine. Each class of languages has its own quirks and emphasis, and no single engine will handle all the different types of languages well. Trying to design an engine that works equally well for all languages will get you an engine that executes all of them poorly.

That doesn't mean that we've ignored languages outside our area of primary focus—far from it. We've worked hard to make sure that we can accommodate as many languages as possible without compromising the performance of our core language set. We feel that even though we may not run Prolog or Scheme code as fast as a dedicated engine would, the flexibility Parrot provides to mix and match languages more than makes up for that.

Parrot's core design is that of a register rich CISC CPU, like many of the CISC machines of the past such as the VAX, Motorola 68000, and IBM System/3x0. Many of the core opcodes—Parrot's basic instructions—perform complex operations. It also bears some resemblance to modern RISC CPUs such as the IBM Power series and Intel Alpha,[*] as it does all its operations on data in registers. Using a core design similar to older systems gives us decades of compiler research to draw on. Most compiler research since the early 1970s deals with targeting register systems of one sort or another.

Using a register architecture as the basis for Parrot goes against the current trends in virtual machines, which favor stack-based approaches. While a stack approach is simpler to implement, a register system provides a richer set of semantics. It's also just more pleasant for us assembly old-timers to write code for. Combined with the decades of sophisticated compiler research, we feel that it's the correct design decision.

Registers

Parrot has four basic types of registers: PMC, string, integer, and floating-point, one for each of the core data types in Parrot. We separate them out for ease of implementation, garbage collection, and space efficiency. Since

---

[*] Formerly HP, formerly Compaq, formerly Digital Alpha.

PMCs and strings are garbage-collectable entities, restricting what can access them—strings in string registers and PMCs in PMC registers—makes the garbage collector a bit faster and simpler. Having integers and floats in separate register sets makes sense from a space standpoint, since floats are normally larger than integers.

The current Parrot architecture provides 32 of each register type, for a total of 128 registers. While this may seem like overkill, compensating for running out of registers can be a significant speed hit, so it's in our best interests to make sure it happens rarely. 32 is a good compromise between performance and memory usage.

Stacks

Parrot has seven separate stacks, each with a specific purpose. The four register sets each have its own stack for quickly saving register contents. There is a separate stack dedicated to saving and restoring individual integers, which the regular expression system uses heavily. The control stack keeps track of control information, exception handlers, and other such things. Finally, the general-purpose typed stack stores individual values.

The backing stacks for the register sets are somewhat special. Operations on the register stacks don't act on single registers. The engine pushes and pops entire register sets in one operation. This may seem somewhat unusual, but it makes the primary use of these stacks—to save registers across function calls—very fast. A save or restore operation is essentially a single memory copy operation, something that's highly optimized just about everywhere.*

The integer stack is specifically designed to hold integers. Since it doesn't have to be general purpose, integer stack operations can be faster than operations on the general-purpose stack—a speed gain the regular expression code makes use of. Regular expressions make heavy use of integer code, as they move back and forth within strings, and make heavy use of the integer stack to manage backtracking information.

The control stack is private to the interpreter, so user code can't directly access it. The interpreter engine uses it to manage exception handlers, return locations for function calls, and track other internal data. User code can inspect the stack through Parrot's introspective features.

Finally, the general-purpose stack is used to save and restore individual registers. It's a typed stack, so it doesn't allow you to do things like push an

---

* The SPARC processor, for example, has a cache-friendly memory copy as a core operation.

integer register onto the stack and pop the value into a string register. For compiled code, this stack is used if a routine needs more than 32 registers of the same type. The extra values are pushed on and popped off the stack in an operation called register spilling. This stack is also used when Parrot runs code designed for a stack machine such as the JVM or .NET. Stack-based code is less efficient than register-based code, but we can still run it.

All of Parrot's stacks are segmented—they're composed of a set of stack pieces instead of a single chunk of memory. Segmenting has a small performance impact, but it allows us to make better usage of available memory. Traditional stacks are composed of a single chunk of memory, since this makes it faster to read from and write to the stack. Usually when you run off the end of that chunk of memory your program crashes. To avoid this, most systems allocate a large stack. This isn't much of a problem if you have only a single stack, but it doesn't work well in today's multithreaded world, where each thread has to have its own stack.

Another pleasant benefit of segmenting the stacks is that it makes supporting coroutines and continuations much easier. It is much easier to save off part of a segmented stack. Combined with Parrot's copy-on-write features, this makes for efficient continuations and coroutines. It may not be a feature that many folks will use, but it's a pleasant fall-out from other things.

Strings

Text data is deceptively complex, so Parrot has strings as a fundamental data type. We do this out of sheer practicality. We know strings are complex and error-prone, so we implement them only once. All languages that target Parrot can share the same implementation, and don't have to make their own mistakes.

The big problem with text is the vast number of human languages and the variety of conventions around the world for dealing with it. Long ago, 7-bit ASCII with 127 characters was sufficient. Computers were limited and mostly used in English, regardless of the user's native language. These heavy restrictions were acceptable because the machines of the day were so limited that any other option was too slow. Also, most people using computers at the time were fluent in English either as their native language or a comfortable second language.

That day passed quite a few years ago. Many different ways of representing text have sprung up, from the various multibyte Japanese and Chinese representations—designed for languages with many thousands of characters—to a half dozen or so European representations, which take only a byte but disagree on what characters fit into that byte. The Unicode consortium has been working for years on the Unicode standard to try and unify all the different schemes, but full unification is years away, if it ever happens.

In the abstract, strings are a series of integers with meaning attached to them, but getting from real-world data to abstract integers isn't as simple as you might want. There are three important things associated with string data—encoding, character set, and language—and Parrot's string system knows how to deal with them.

A string's *encoding* says how to turn data from a stream of bytes to a stream of characters represented by integers. Something like ASCII data is simple to deal with, since each character is a single byte, and characters range in value from 0 to 255. UTF-8, one of the Unicode encodings, is more complex—a single character can take anywhere from 1 to 6 bytes.

The *character set* for a string tells Parrot what each of the integers actually represents. Parrot won't get too far if it doesn't know that 65 is a capital "A" in an ASCII or Unicode character stream, for example.

Finally, the *language* for a string determines how the string behaves in some contexts. Different languages have different rules for sorting and case-folding characters. Whether an accented character keeps its accent when uppercased or lowercased depends on the language that the string came from.

The capability of translating strings from one encoding to another and one character set to another, and to determine when it's needed, is built into Parrot. The I/O and regular expression systems fully exploit Parrot's core string capabilities, so any language that uses Parrot's built-in string functionality gets this for free. Since properly implementing even a single system like Unicode is fraught with peril, this makes the job of people writing languages that target Parrot (including Perl 6) much easier.

Variables

Variables are a fundamental construct in almost all computer languages.[*] With low-level languages such as C, variables are straightforward—they are either basic hardware constructs like a 32-bit integer, a 64-bit IEEE floating-point number, or the address of some location in memory, or they're a structure containing basic hardware constructs. Exchanging variables between low-level languages is simple because all the languages operate on essentially the same things.

---

[*] With the exception of functional languages, though they can be useful there as well.

Once you get to higher-level languages, variables get more interesting. OO languages have the concept of the object as a fundamental construct, but no two OO languages seem to agree on exactly how objects should behave or how they should be implemented. Then there are higher-level languages like Perl, with complex constructs like hashes, arrays, and polymorphic scalars as fundamental constructs.

The first big issue that Parrot had to face was implementing these constructs. The second was doing it in a way that allowed Perl code to use Ruby objects, Ruby code to use Python objects, and Lisp code to use both. Parrot's solution is the PMC, or Parrot Magic Cookie.

A PMC is an abstract variable and a base data type—the same way that integers and floating-point numbers are base data types for hardware CPUs. The languages we're working to support—Perl, Python, and Ruby—have base variables that are far more complex than just an integer or floating-point number. If we want them to exchange any sort of real data, they must have a common base variable type. Parrot provides that with the PMC construct. Each language can build on this common base. More importantly, each language can make sure that their variables behave properly regardless of which language is using them.

When you think about it, there is a large list of things that a variable should be able to do. You should, for example, be able to load or store a value, add or subtract it from another variable, call a method or set a property on it, get its integer or floating-point representation, and so on. What we did was make a list of these functions and make them mandatory.

Each PMC has a vtable, a table of function pointers, attached to it. This table is fixed. The list of functions, and where they are in the table, is the same for each PMC. All the common operations a program might perform on a variable—as well as all the operators that might be overloaded for a PMC—have vtable entries.

Bytecode

Like any CPU, software, or hardware, Parrot needs a set of instructions to tell it what to do. For hardware, this is a stream of executable code or machine language. For Parrot, this is bytecode. Calling it bytecode isn't strictly accurate, since the individual instructions are 32 bits each rather than 8 bits each, but since it's the common term for most other virtual machines, it's the term we use.

Each instruction—also known as an "opcode"—tells the interpreter engine what to do. Some opcodes are very low level, such as the one to add two integers together. Others are significantly more complex, like the opcode to take a continuation.

Parrot's bytecode is designed to be directly executable. The code on disk can be run by the interpreter without needing any translation. This gets us a number of benefits. Loading is much faster, of course, since we don't have to do much (if any) processing on the bytecode as it's loaded. It also means we can use some special OS calls that map a file directly into the memory space of a process. Because of the way this is handled by the operating system,* the bytecode file will be loaded into the system's memory only once, no matter how many processes use the file. This can save a significant amount of real RAM on server systems. Files loaded this way also get their parts loaded on demand. Since we don't need to process the bytecode in any way to execute it, if you map in a large bytecode library file, only those bits of the file your program actually executes will get read in from disk. This can save a lot of time.

Parrot creates bytecode in a format optimized for the platform it's built on, since the common case by far is executing bytecode that's been built on the system you're using. This means that floating-point numbers are stored in the current platform's native format, integers are in the native size, and both are stored in the byte order for the current platform. Parrot does have the capability of executing bytecode that uses 32-bit integers and IEEE floating-point numbers on any platform, so you can build and ship bytecode that can be run by anyone with a Parrot interpreter.

If you do use a bytecode file that doesn't match the current platform's requirements (perhaps the integers are a different size), Parrot automatically translates the bytecode file as it reads it in. In this case, Parrot does have to read in the entire file and process it. The sharing and load speed benefits are lost, but it's a small price to pay for the portability. Parrot ships with a utility to turn a portable bytecode file into a native format bytecode file if the overhead is too onerous.

I/O, Events, Signals, and Threads

Parrot has comprehensive support for I/O, threads, and events. These three systems are interrelated, so we'll treat them together. The systems we talk about in this section are less mature than other parts of the engine, so they may change by the time we roll out the final design and implementation.

---

* Conveniently, this works the same way for all the flavors of Unix, Windows, and VMS.

I/O

Parrot's base I/O system is fully asynchronous I/O with callbacks and per-request private data. Since this is massive overkill in many cases, we have a plain vanilla synchronous I/O layer that your programs can use if they don't need the extra power.

Asynchronous I/O is conceptually pretty simple. Your program makes an I/O request. The system takes that request and returns control to your program, which keeps running. Meanwhile the system works on satisfying the I/O request. When the request is satisfied, the system notifies your program in some way. Since there can be multiple requests outstanding, and you can't be sure exactly what your program will be doing when a request is satisfied, programs that make use of asynchronous I/O can be complex.

Synchronous I/O is even simpler. Your program makes a request to the system and then waits until that request is done. There can be only one request in process at a time, and you always know what you're doing (waiting) while the request is being processed. It makes your program much simpler, since you don't have to do any sort of coordination or synchronization.

The big benefit of asynchronous I/O systems is that they generally have a much higher throughput than a synchronous system. They move data around much faster—in some cases three or four times faster. This is because the system can be busy moving data to or from disk while your program is busy processing data that it got from a previous request.

For disk devices, having multiple outstanding requests—especially on a busy system—allows the system to order read and write requests to take better advantage of the underlying hardware. For example, many disk devices have built-in track buffers. No matter how small a request you make to the drive, it always reads a full track. With synchronous I/O, if your program makes two small requests to the same track, and they're separated by a request for some other data, the disk will have to read the full track twice. With asynchronous I/O, on the other hand, the disk may be able to read the track just once, and satisfy the second request from the track buffer.

Parrot's I/O system revolves around a request. A request has three parts: a buffer for data, a completion routine, and a piece of data private to the request. Your program issues the request, then goes about its business. When the request is completed, Parrot will call the completion routine, passing it the request that just finished. The completion routine extracts out the buffer and the private data, and does whatever it needs to do to handle the request. If your request doesn't have a completion routine, then your program will have to explicitly check to see if the request was satisfied.

Your program can choose to sleep and wait for the request to finish, essentially blocking. Parrot will continue to process events while your program is waiting, so it isn't completely unresponsive. This is how Parrot implements synchronous I/O—it issues the asynchronous request, then immediately waits for that request to complete.

The reason we made Parrot's I/O system asynchronous by default was sheer pragmatism. Network I/O is all asynchronous, as is GUI programming, so we knew we had to deal with asynchrony in some form. It's also far easier to make an asynchronous system pretend to be synchronous than it is the other way around. We could have decided to treat GUI events, network I/O, and file I/O all separately, but there are plenty of systems around that demonstrate what a bad idea that is.

Events

An event is a notification that something has happened: the user has manipulated a GUI element, an I/O request has completed, a signal has been triggered, or a timer has expired. Most systems these days have an event handler,* because handling events is so fundamental to modern GUI programming. Unfortunately, the event handling system is not integrated, or poorly integrated, with the I/O system, leading to nasty code and unpleasant workarounds to try and make a program responsive to network, file, and GUI events simultaneously. Parrot presents a unified event handling system, integrated with its I/O system, which makes it possible to write cross-platform programs that work well in a complex environment.

Parrot's events are fairly simple. An event has an event type, some event data, an event handler, and a priority. Each thread has an event queue, and when an event happens it's put into the right thread's queue (or the default thread queue in those cases where we can't tell which thread an event was destined for) to wait for something to process it.

Any operation that would potentially block drains the event queue while it waits, as do a number of the cleanup opcodes that Parrot uses to tidy up on scope exit. Parrot doesn't check each opcode for an outstanding event for pure performance reasons, as that check gets expensive quickly. Still, Parrot generally ensures timely event handling, and events shouldn't sit in a queue for more than a few milliseconds unless event handling has been explicitly disabled.

---

* Often two or three, which is something of a problem.

When Parrot does extract an event from the event queue, it calls that event's event handler, if it has one. If an event doesn't have a handler, Parrot instead looks for a generic handler for the event type and calls it instead. If for some reason there's no handler for the event type, Parrot falls back to the generic event handler, which throws an exception when it gets an event it doesn't know how to handle. You can override the generic event handler if you want Parrot to do something else with unhandled events, perhaps silently discarding them instead.

Because events are handled in mainline code, they don't have the restrictions commonly associated with interrupt-level code. It's safe and acceptable for an event handler to throw an exception, allocate memory, or manipulate thread or global state safely. Event handlers can even acquire locks if they need to, though it's not a good idea to have an event handler blocking on lock acquisition.

Parrot uses the priority on events for two purposes. First, the priority is used to order the events in the event queue. Events for a particular priority are handled in a FIFO manner, but higher-priority events are always handled before lower-priority events. Parrot also allows a user program or event handler to set a minimum event priority that it will handle. If an event with a priority lower than the current minimum arrives, it won't be handled, instead sitting in the queue until the minimum priority level is dropped. This allows an event handler that's dealing with a high-priority event to ignore lower-priority events.

User code generally doesn't need to deal with prioritized events, so programmers should adjust event priorities with care. Adjusting the default priority of an event, or adjusting the current minimum priority level, is a rare occurrence. It's almost always a mistake to change them, but the capability is there for those rare occasions where it's the correct thing to do.

Signals

Signals are a special form of event, based on the Unix signal mechanism. Parrot presents them as mildly special, as a remnant of Perl's Unix heritage, but under the hood they're not treated any differently from any other event.

The Unix signaling mechanism is something of a mash, having been extended and worked on over the years by a small legion of undergrad programmers. At this point, signals can be divided into two categories, those that are fatal, and those that aren't.

Fatal signals are things like SIGKILL, which unconditionally kills a process, or SIGBUS, which indicates that the process has tried to access memory that isn't part of your process. There's no good way for Parrot to catch these signals, so they remain fatal and will kill your process. On some systems it may be possible to catch some of the fatal signals, but Parrot code itself operates at too high a level for a user program to do anything with them—they must be handled with special-purpose code written in C or some other low-level language. Parrot itself may catch them in special circumstances for its own use, but that's an implementation detail that isn't exposed to a user program.

Non-fatal signals are things like SIGCHLD, indicating that a child process has died, or SIGTERM, indicating that the user has hit ^C on the keyboard. Parrot turns these signals into events and puts them in the event queue. Your program's event handler for the signal will be called as soon as Parrot gets to the event in the queue, and your code can do what it needs to with it.

SIGALRM, which indicates that a timer has expired, is often treated specially in user code. A process could only have one timer going, and on many Unix systems this used to be the only way to set a timeout on I/O operations that may potentially block forever, and many Perl programs use it as such. Parrot's async I/O system can't block forever, allows you to abort any outstanding I/O request, and the event system allows you to have as many timer events as you want outstanding, so handling it is much less necessary than it used to be.

Threads

Threads are a means of splitting a process into multiple pieces that execute simultaneously. It's a relatively easy way to get some parallelism without too much work. Threads don't solve all the parallelism problems your program may have. Sometimes multiple processes on a single system, multiple processes on a cluster, or processes on multiple separate systems are better. But threads do present a good solution for many common cases.

All the resources in a threaded process are shared between threads. This is simultaneously the great strength and great weakness of threads. Easy sharing is fast sharing, making it far faster to exchange data between threads or access shared global data than to share data between processes on a single system or on multiple systems. Easy sharing is dangerous, though, since without some sort of coordination between threads it's easy to corrupt that shared data. And, because all the threads are contained within a single process, if any one of them fails for some reason the entire process, with all its threads, dies.

With a low-level language such as C, these issues are manageable. The core data types, integers, floats, and pointers are all small enough to be handled atomically. Composite data can be protected with mutexes, special structures that a thread can get exclusive access to. The composite data elements that need protecting can each have a mutex associated with them, and when a thread needs to touch the data it just acquires the mutex first. By default there's very little data that must be shared between threads, so it's relatively easy, barring program errors, to write thread-safe code if a little thought is given to the program structure.

Things aren't this easy for Parrot, unfortunately. A PMC, Parrot's native data type, is a complex structure, so we can't count on the hardware to provide us atomic access. That means Parrot has to provide atomicity itself, which is expensive. Getting and releasing a mutex isn't really that expensive in itself. It has been heavily optimized by platform vendors because they want threaded code to run quickly. It's not free, though, and when you consider that running flat-out Parrot does one PMC operation per 100 CPU cycles, even adding an additional 10 cycles per operation can slow Parrot down by 10%.

For any threading scheme, it's important that your program isn't hindered by the platform and libraries it uses. This is a common problem with writing threaded code in C, for example. Many libraries you might use aren't thread-safe, and if you aren't careful with them your program will crash. While we can't make low-level libraries any safer, we can make sure that Parrot itself won't be a danger. There is very little data shared between Parrot interpreters and threads, and access to all the shared data is done with coordinating mutexes. This is invisible to your program, and just makes sure that Parrot itself is thread-safe.

When you think about it, there are really three different threading models. In the first one, multiple threads have no interaction among themselves. This essentially does with threads the same thing that's done with processes. This works very well in Parrot, with the isolation between interpreters helping to reduce the overhead of this scheme. There's no possibility of data sharing at the user level, so there's no need to lock anything.

In the second threading model, multiple threads run and pass messages back and forth between each other. Parrot supports this as well, via the event mechanism. The event queues are thread-safe, so one thread can safely inject an event into another thread's event queue. This is similar to a multiple-process model of programming, except that communication between threads is much faster, and it's easier to pass around structured data.

In the third threading model, multiple threads run and share data between themselves. While Parrot can't guarantee that data at the user level remains consistent, it can make sure that access to shared data is at least safe. We do this with two mechanisms.

First, Parrot presents an advisory lock system to user code. Any piece of user code running in a thread can lock a variable. Any attempt to lock a variable that another thread has locked will block until the lock is released. Locking a variable only blocks other lock attempts. It does *not* block plain access. This may seem odd, but it's the same scheme used by threading systems that obey the POSIX thread standard, and has been well tested in practice.

Secondly, Parrot forces all shared PMCs to be marked as such, and all access to shared PMCs must first acquire that PMC's private lock. This is done by installing an alternate vtable for shared PMCs, one that acquires locks on all its parameters. These locks are held only for the duration of the vtable function, but ensure that the PMCs affected by the operation aren't altered by another thread while the vtable function is in progress.

Objects

Perl 5, Perl 6, Python, and Ruby are all object-oriented languages in some form or other, so Parrot has to have core support for objects and classes. Unfortunately, all these languages have somewhat different object systems, which made the design of Parrot's object system somewhat tricky.* It turns out that if you draw the abstraction lines in the right places, support for the different systems is easily possible. This is especially true if you provide core support for things like method dispatch that the different object systems can use and override.

Generic Object Interfacing

Parrot's object system is very simple—in fact, a PMC only has to handle method calls to be considered an object. Just handling methods covers well over 90% of the object functionality that most programs use, since the vast majority of object access is via method calls. This means that user code that does the following:

```
object = some_constructor(1, 2, "foo");
object.bar(12);
```

will work just fine, no matter what language the class that backs object is written in, if object even has a class backing it. It could be Perl 5, Perl 6, Python, Ruby, or even Java, C#, or Common Lisp; it doesn't matter.

---

* As I write this it's still in progress, though it should be done by the time this book is in print.

Objects may override other functionality as well. For example, Python objects use the basic PMC property mechanism to implement object attributes. Both Python and Perl 6 mandate that methods and properties share the same namespace, with methods overriding properties of the same name.

Parrot Objects

When we refer to Parrot objects we're really talking about Parrot's default base object type. Any PMC type that implements the method call vtable entry is an object as far as Parrot is concerned, but while that's sufficient to use an object, it's not enough to make the objects actually work.

Parrot's standard object uses a slot-based attribute model. Each object is essentially a small array, with one element per attribute in the object's class and superclasses. Each object carries a directory of which slots are used by which classes for which attributes. This allows introspective data browsers to show objects at runtime and runtime additions of attributes to objects.

Parrot's standard object and its base class aren't particularly special, and certainly not the optimal universal object type. Its characteristics were chosen to meet the needs of the Perl 6 object system, though it should suffice as a base type for Ruby, Python, Java, and .NET objects.

Parrot Classes

As with objects, Parrot requires some base functionality of classes. Unlike objects, which have a required action (the method call), classes have required metadata. Since Parrot classes are themselves PMCs, the required metadata is stored as properties on the class PMCs. Classes may also reserve a section of the namespace and define subs and methods in that namespace, but that's not strictly required.

To conform to Parrot's standards, a class must expose a class type property. This property specifies whether the class is a subclass of Parrot's base object class, a class that isn't a subclass of Parrot's base class but is still available for inheritance, or an opaque class that can't be subclassed by Parrot's base class.*

Opaque classes are easy. We just ignore them and assume that their internal code (or code emitted by the languages that use them) know how to manipulate, subclass, and otherwise fiddle with them. Generic Parrot code inspectors won't be able to dive into them, but that's not necessarily a bad thing. You wouldn't expect to look at the source for a C++ class from within Parrot.

---

* Remember, Parrot supports multiple inheritance.

Parrot's base class is also simple enough to handle. Since we have full control over it, Parrot can peek and cheat as needed. The base class, as you've seen, is based on an attribute array model and comes with a set of default methods for method dispatch, property fetching, etc.

Inheritable classes that aren't based on Parrot's base class are another matter entirely. Parrot supports them with transparent delegation, as we'll see in the next section. The classes themselves don't have to do much to get this support. A non-base inheritable class must set properties on the class object that tell Parrot where to find its allocation and initialization methods. It also must make sure on method dispatch that the object isn't really a delegated part of a containing object. The engine provides code to do this efficiently.

Mixed Class-Type Support

The final piece of Parrot's object system is the support for inheriting from classes of different types. This could be a Perl 6 class inheriting from a Perl 5 class, or a Ruby class inheriting from a .NET class. It could even involve inheriting from a fully compiled language such as C++ or Objective C, if proper wrapping is established.*

As we talked about earlier, as long as a class either descends from the base Parrot class or has a small number of required properties, Parrot can subclass it. This potentially goes both ways, as any class system that knows how to subclass from Parrot's base class can inherit from it.

Allowing classes to inherit from other classes of a different base type does present some interesting technical issues. The inheritance isn't 100% invisible, though you have to head off into the corner cases to find the cracks. It's an important feature to design into Parrot, so we can subclass Perl 5 style classes, and they can subclass Parrot classes. Being able to subclass C++ and Objective C classes is a potential bonus. Python, Ruby, and Perl 6 all share a common (but hidden) base class in Parrot's base object type, so they can inherit from each other without difficulty.

Advanced Features

Since the languages Parrot targets (like Perl and Ruby) have sophisticated concepts as core features, it's in Parrot's best interest to have core support for them. This section covers some (but not all) of these features.

---

* Objective C is particularly simple, as it has a fully introspective class system that allows for runtime class creation. Inheritance can go both ways between it and Parrot.

Garbage Collection

It's expected that modern languages have garbage collection built in. The programmer shouldn't have to worry about explicitly cleaning up after dead variables, or even identifying them. For interpreted languages, this requires support from the interpreter engine, so Parrot provides that support.

Parrot has two separate allocation systems built into it. Each allocation system has its own garbage collection scheme. Parrot also has some strict rules over what can be referenced and from where. This allows it to have a more efficient garbage collection system.

The first allocation system is responsible for PMC and string structures. These are fixed-sized objects that Parrot allocates out of arenas, which are pools of identically sized things. Using arenas makes it easy for Parrot to find and track them, and speeds up the detection of dead objects.

Parrot's dead object detection system works by first running through all the arenas and marking all strings and PMCs as dead. It then runs through the stacks and registers, marking all strings and PMCs they reference as alive. Next, it iteratively runs through all the live PMCs and strings and marks everything they reference as alive. Finally, it sweeps through all the arenas looking for newly dead PMCs and strings, which it puts on the free list. At this point, any PMC that has a custom destruction routine, such as an object with a DESTROY method, has its destruction routine called. The dead object detector is triggered whenever Parrot runs out of free objects, and can be explicitly triggered by running code. Often a language compiler will force a dead object sweep when leaving a block or subroutine.

Parrot's memory allocation system is used to allocate space for the contents of strings and PMCs. Allocations don't have a fixed size; they come from pools of memory that Parrot maintains. Whenever Parrot runs out of memory in its memory pools, it makes a compacting run—squeezing out unused sections from the pools. When it's done, one end of each pool is entirely actively used memory, and the other end is one single chunk of free memory. This makes allocating memory from the pools faster, as there's no need to walk a free list looking for a segment of memory large enough to satisfy the request for memory. It also makes more efficient use of memory, as there's less overhead than in a traditional memory allocation system.

Splitting memory pool compaction from dead object detection has a nice performance benefit for Perl and languages like it. For most Perl programs, the interpreter allocates and reallocates far more memory for string and variable contents than it does actual string and variable structures. The structures are reused over and over as their contents change. With a traditional single-collector system, each time the interpreter runs out of memory it has to do a full scan for dead objects and compact the pools after. With a split system, Parrot can just sweep through the variables it thinks are live and compact their contents. This does mean that Parrot will sometimes move data for variables and strings that are really dead because it hasn't found that out yet. That expense is normally much less than the expense of doing a full tracing run to find out which variables are actually dead.

Parrot's allocation and collection systems have some compromises that make interfacing with low-level code easier. The structure that describes a PMC or string is guaranteed not to move over the lifetime of the string or variable. This allows C code to store pointers to variables in internal structures without worrying that what they're referencing may move. It also means that the garbage collection system doesn't have to worry about updating pointers that C code might hold, which it would have to do if PMC or string structures could move.

Signature-Based Dispatching

Signature-based dispatching, or multimethod dispatching, is a powerful technique that uses the parameters of a function or method call to help decide at runtime what function or method Parrot should call. This is one of the new features being built into Perl 6. It allows you to have two or more subroutines or methods with the same name that differ only in the types of their arguments. At runtime Parrot looks at the parameters for a subroutine or method call and figures out what the best subroutine or method to call is.

This allows for some very powerful behaviors, as well as giving a good opportunity for optimization. For example, take the following three lines of code:

```
$a = 1 + 2;
$b = 1 + 2.0;
$c = 1 + "2";
```

The result is the same in each case—all the variables end up with a value of 3. But each of those three statements needs to execute different code.

In the first case, it's plain integer addition, which is the fastest possible way. The math itself probably takes a single CPU cycle. The second case adds an integer to a floating-point value, something that requires different code than adding two integers does. In the third case, we need to turn one of the arguments from a string into a number.

In this example we can easily figure out at compile time which kind of addition code to use. If the code was instead something like:

```
$a = $b + $c;
```

we couldn't know at compile time what kind of addition was needed. We have to check at runtime, and do the right kind of math based on the types of the two arguments.

Multimethod dispatch is also very useful for normal subroutines and methods. You've probably found yourself writing code that checks the types of its arguments and does different things based on what types are passed in, something like:

```
sub foo {
    my ($self, $arg) = @_;
    if ($arg->isa("Thing")) {
        #...
    } elsif ($arg->isa("OtherThing")) {
        #...
    } elsif ($arg->isa("Doodad")) {
        #...
    } else {
        #...
    }
}
```

This is a manual form of multimethod dispatch. If you've done it, you no doubt found that once you get past three or four different checks, the code becomes very unwieldy and hard to maintain. Using multimethods, you do the same thing with three or four methods that you don't have to check at all, as the system does it for you.

Finally, multimethod dispatch provides a way to carefully inject code into another package, which is especially useful when dealing with overloaded operators. It's not at all uncommon to have a data type that behaves differently depending on whether it's on the left or right side of an operator. Normally, the data on the left-hand side of an operator controls the operation. If you're adding a new data type such as a matrix, the code for the data type on the left-hand side of the operator won't know about your new type, so it can't perform the operation properly. Using multimethod dispatch, and allowing code to add in new variants of a function or method at runtime, makes it much more likely that your program will get the correct answer.

Continuations

Continuations are possibly the most powerful high-level flow control construct. Originating with lambda calculus, and built into Lisp over thirty years ago, continuations can be thought of as a closure for control flow. They not only capture their lexical scope, which gets restored when they're invoked, but also capture their call stack, so when they're invoked it's as if you never left the spot where they were created.

Continuations are phenomenally powerful, but with great power comes great confusion. Indeed, some languages specifically designed to be as obfuscated as possible include continuations just because they're so mind-warping. Still, you can duplicate any control structure you can think of with continuations, and there are times when their power is necessary to do some advanced things. Because of this, and because Ruby provides them as core functionality, Parrot has support for them.

Interestingly, this did trigger a number of other useful features. Efficient continuation support requires a framed, segmented call stack and copy-on-write semantics for interpreter control structures. These are very useful for threads, efficient string usage, and coroutines, so the feature was well worth it. It also allows Parrot to provide all the semantics necessary for an interoperable Scheme implementation, which is a good thing as well.

Coroutines

A coroutine is a subroutine or method that can suspend itself partway through, then later pick up where it left off. This isn't quite the same thing as a continuation, though it may seem so at first. Coroutines are often used to implement iterators and generators, as well as threads on systems that don't have native threading support. Since they are so useful, and since Perl 6 and Python provide them either directly or as generators, Parrot has support for them built in.

Coroutines present some interesting technical challenges. Calling into an existing coroutine requires reestablishing not only the lexical state and potentially the hypothetical state of variables, but also the control state for just the routine. Coroutines can be implemented in terms of continuations if need be, but that requires using a full continuation-passing function call system, something we chose not to do.

Conclusion

We've touched on much of Parrot's core functionality, but certainly not all. Hopefully we've given you enough of a feel for how Parrot works to expand your knowledge with the Parrot documentation and source.

## CHAPTER 6

Parrot Assembly Language

Owner: Sorry squire, I've had a look 'round
the back of the shop, and uh,
we're right out of parrots.
Customer: I see. I see, I get the picture.
Owner: <pause> I got a slug.
—Monty Python's Flying Circus
  "Parrot Sketch"

Parrot assembly (PASM) is an assembly language written for Parrot's virtual CPU. PASM has an interesting mix of features. Because it's an assembly language, it has many low-level features, such as flow control based on branches and jumps, and direct manipulation of values on the software registers and stacks. Basic register operations or branches are generally a single CPU instruction.* On the other hand, because it's designed to implement dynamic high-level languages, it has support for many advanced features, such as lexical and global variables, objects, garbage collection, continuations, coroutines, and much more.

Getting Started

The first step before you start playing with PASM code is to get a copy of the source code and compile it. There is some information on this in "Use the source" in Chapter 2. For more information and updates, see *http://www. parrotcode.org* and the documentation in the distributed code.

---

* This means the JIT runtime has a performance of one PASM instruction per processor cycle.

The basic steps are:[*]

```
$ perl Configure.pl
$ make
$ make test
```

With versions of Parrot later than 0.0.10, you can speed up the testing process significantly by compiling IMCC first (see "Getting Started") and running the tests with IMCC instead of the Parrot assembler:

```
$ make test IMCC=languages/imcc/imcc
```

Once you've compiled Parrot, create a small test file in the main *parrot* directory. We'll call it *fjord.pasm*.

```
print "He's pining for the fjords.\n"
end
```

.pasm is the standard extension for Parrot assembly language source files. Compile it to bytecode, using *assemble.pl*:

```
$ ./assemble.pl fjord.pasm --output fjord.pbc
```

You specify the name of the output bytecode file with the --output (or -o) switch. *.pbc* is the standard extension for Parrot bytecode. Finally, run the compiled bytecode file through the *parrot* interpreter:

```
$ ./parrot fjord.pbc
```

That's all there is to it.[†] If you're anything like me, the next thing you're going to do is symlink *parrot* from a directory in your PATH, and write a tiny script for the assembler so that from any directory you can just type:

```
$ assemble fjord.pasm
$ parrot fjord.pbc
```

These last steps are optional. In fact, something similar may be done for you with a make install target by the time you read this.

Basics

PASM has a simple syntax. Each statement stands on its own line. Statements begin with a Parrot instruction code (commonly referred to as an "opcode"). The arguments follow, separated by commas:

```
[label] opcode dest, source, source ...
```

---

[*] Not all operating systems have *make*. Check the documentation for instructions for systems that aren't Unix-based.

[†] Though you may want to look ahead to "Getting Started" in Chapter 7 for a one-step way to run PASM code.

If the opcode returns a result, it is stored in the first argument. Sometimes the first register is both a source value and the destination of the operation. The arguments are either registers or constants, though only source arguments can be constants:

```
LABEL:
    print "The answer is: "
    print 42
    print "\n"
    end                 # halt the interpreter
```

Comments are marked with the hash sign (#) and continue to the end of the line. Any line can start with a label definition like LABEL:, but label definitions can also stand on their own line.

Constants

Integer constants are signed integers.* Integer constants can have a positive (+) or negative (-) sign in front. Binary integers are preceded by 0b or 0B, and hexadecimal integers are preceded by 0x or 0X:

```
print 42          # integer constant
print -0b101      # binary integer constant with sign
print 0Xdeadbeef  # hex integer constant
```

Floating-point constants can also be positive or negative. Scientific notation provides an exponent, marked with e or E (the sign of the exponent is optional):

```
print 3.14159     # floating point constant
print -1.23e+45   # in scientific notation
```

String constants are wrapped in single or double quotation marks. Quotation marks and other nonprintable characters inside the string have to be escaped by a backslash. The escape sequences for special characters are the same as for Perl 5's qq( ) operator.

```
print "string\n"    # string constant with escaped newline
print 'that\'s it'  # escaped single quote
print "\\"          # a literal backslash
```

Working with Registers

Parrot is a register-based virtual machine. It has 4 typed register sets with 32 registers in each set. The types are integers, floating-point numbers, strings,

---

* The size of integers is defined when Parrot is configured. It's typically 32 bits on 32-bit machines (a range of -2^{31} to $+2^{31-1}$) and twice that size on 64-bit processors.

and Parrot objects. Register names consist of a capital letter indicating the register set and the number of the register, between 0 and 31. For example:

```
I0    integer register #0
N11   number or floating point register #11
S2    string register #2
P31   PMC register #31
```

Integer and number registers hold values, while string and PMC registers contain pointers to allocated memory for a string header or a Parrot object.

The length of strings is limited only by your system's virtual memory and by the size of integers on the particular platform. Parrot can work with strings of different character types and encodings. It automatically converts string operands with mixed characteristics to Unicode.*

Parrot Magic Cookies (PMCs) are Parrot's low-level objects. They can represent data of any arbitrary type. The operations (methods) for each PMC class are defined in a fixed vtable, which is a structure containing function pointers that implement each operation.

Register assignment

The most basic operation on registers is assignment using the set opcode:

```
set I0, 42        # set integer register #0 to the integer value 42
set N3, 3.14159   # set number register #3 to the value of π
set I1, I0        # set register I1 to what I0 contains
set I2, N3        # cast the floating point number to an integer
```

PASM uses registers where a high-level language would use variables. The exchange opcode swaps the contents of two registers of the same type:

```
exchange I1, I0   # set register I1 to what I0 contains
                  # and set register I0 to what I1 contains
```

As we mentioned before, string and PMC registers are slightly different because they hold a pointer instead of directly holding a value. Assigning one string register to another:

```
set S0, "Ford"
set S1, S0
set S0, "Zaphod"
print S1                # prints "Ford"
end
```

doesn't make a copy of the string; it makes a copy of the pointer. Just after set S1, S0, both S0 and S1 point to the same string. But assigning a constant

---

* This conversion isn't fully implemented yet.

string to a string register allocates a new string. When "Zaphod" is assigned to S0, the pointer changes to point to the location of the new string, leaving the old string untouched. So strings act like simple values on the user level, even though they're implemented as pointers.

Unlike strings, assignment to a PMC doesn't automatically create a new object; it only calls the PMC's vtable method for assignment. So, rewriting the same example using a PMC has a completely different result:

```
new P0, .PerlString
set P0, "Ford"
set P1, P0
set P0, "Zaphod"
print P1                # prints "Zaphod"
end
```

The new opcode creates an instance of the .PerlString class. The class's vtable methods define how the PMC in P0 operates. The first set statement calls P0's vtable method set_string_native, which assigns the string "Ford" to the PMC. When P0 is assigned to P1:

```
set P1, P0
```

it copies the pointer, so P1 are P0 both aliases to the same PMC. Then, assigning the string "Zaphod" to P0 changes the underlying PMC, so printing P1 or P0 prints "Zaphod".*

PMC object types

Internally, PMC types are represented by positive integers, and built-in types by negative integers. PASM provides two opcodes to deal with types. typeof returns the name corresponding to a numeric type or the type of a PMC. find_type takes a type name and returns the integer value that represents that type.

When the source argument is a PMC and the destination is a string register, typeof returns the name of the type:

```
new P0, .PerlString
typeof S0, P0           # S0 is "PerlString"
print S0
print "\n"
end
```

In this example, typeof returns the type name "PerlString".

---

* Contrast this with assign in "PMC Assignment" later in this chapter.

When the source argument is a PMC and the destination is an integer register, typeof returns the integer representation of the type:

```
new P0, .PerlString
typeof I0, P0              # I0 is 17
print I0
print "\n"
end
```

This example returns the integer representation of PerlString, which is 17.

When typeof's source argument is an integer, it returns the name of the type represented by that integer:

```
set I1, -100
typeof S0, I1             # S0 is "INTVAL"
print S0
print "\n"
end
```

The integer representation of a built-in integer value is −100, so it returns the type name "INTVAL".

The source argument to find_type is always a string containing a type name, and the destination register is always an integer. It returns the integer representation of the type with that name:

```
find_type I1, "PerlString"  # I1 is 17
print I1
print "\n"
find_type I2, "INTVAL"      # I2 is -100
print I2
print "\n"
end
```

Here, the name "PerlString" returns 17, and the name "INTVAL" returns −100.

All Parrot classes inherit from the class default, which has the type number 0. The default class provides some default functionality, but mainly throws exceptions when the default variant of a method is called (meaning the subclass didn't define the method). Type number 0 returns the type name "illegal", since no object should ever be created from the default class:

```
find_type I1, "fancy_super_long_double" # I1 is 0
print I1
print "\n"
typeof S0, I1                           # S0 is "illegal"
print S0
print "\n"
end
```

The type numbers are not fixed values. They change whenever a new class is added to Parrot or when the class hierarchy is altered. A header file containing an enumeration of PMC types (*include/parrot/core_pmcs.h*) is generated during the configuration of the Parrot source tree. The PMC types take their numbers from their order in this file. Internal data types and their names are specified in *include/parrot/datatypes.h*.

You can generate a complete and current list of valid PMC types by running this command within the main Parrot source directory:

```
$ perl classes/pmc2c.pl --tree classes/*.pmc
```

which produces output like:

```
Array
Boolean
    PerlInt
        perlscalar
            scalar
Compiler
    NCI
...
```

The output traces the class hierarchy for each class: `Boolean` inherits from `PerlInt`, which is derived from the abstract `perlscalar` and `scalar` classes (abstract classes are listed in lowercase). The actual classnames and their hierarchy may have changed by the time you read this.

Type morphing

The classes `PerlUndef`, `PerlInt`, `PerlNum`, and `PerlString` implement Perl's polymorphic scalar behavior. Assigning a string to a number PMC morphs it into a string PMC. Assigning an integer value morphs it to a `PerlInt`, and assigning `undef` morphs it to `PerlUndef`:

```
new P0, .PerlString
set P0, "Ford\n"
print P0          # prints "Ford\n"
set P0, 42
print P0          # prints 42
print "\n"
typeof S0, P0
print S0          # prints "PerlInt"
print "\n"
end
```

`P0` is created as a `PerlString`, but when an integer value 42 is assigned to it, it changes to type `PerlInt`.

Math Operations

PASM has a full set of math instructions. These work with integers, floating-point numbers, and PMCs that implement the vtable methods of a numeric object. Most of the major math opcodes have two- and three-argument forms:

```
add I0, I1          # I0 += I1
add I10, I11, I2    # I10 = I11 + I2
```

The three-argument form of add adds the last two numbers and stores the result in the first register. The two-argument form adds the first register to the second and stores the result back in the first register.

The source arguments can be Parrot registers or constants, but they must be compatible with the type of the destination register. Generally, "compatible" means that the source and destination have to be the same type, but there are a few exceptions:

```
sub I0, I1, 2       # I0 = I1 - 2
sub N0, N1, 1.5     # N0 = N1 - 1.5
```

If the destination register is an integer register, like I0, the other arguments must be integer registers or integer constants. A floating-point destination, like N0, usually requires floating-point arguments, but many math opcodes also allow the final argument to be an integer. A PMC destination can have an integer or floating-point argument as the last one:

```
mul P0, P1          # P0 *= P1
mul P0, I1
mul P0, N1
mul P0, P1, P2      # P0 = P1 * P2
mul P0, P1, I2
mul P0, P1, N2
```

Operations on a PMC are implemented by the vtable method of the destination (in the two-argument form) or the left source argument (in the three argument form). The result of an operation is entirely determined by the PMC. A class implementing imaginary number operations might return an imaginary number, for example.

We won't list every math opcode here, but we'll list some of the most common ones. You can get a complete list in "Writing Tests" later in this chapter.

Unary math opcodes

The unary opcodes have a single source argument and a single destination argument. Some of the most common unary math opcodes are inc (increment), dec (decrement), abs (absolute value), neg (negate), and fact (factorial):

```
abs N0, -5.0  # the absolute value of -5.0 is 5.0
fact I1, 5    # the factorial of 5 is 120
inc I1        # 120 incremented by 1 is 121
```

Binary math opcodes

Binary opcodes have two source arguments and a destination argument. As we mentioned before, most binary math opcodes have a two-argument form in which the first argument is both a source and the destination. Parrot provides add (addition), sub (subtraction), mul (multiplication), div (division), and pow (exponent) opcodes, as well as two different modulus operations. mod is Parrot's implementation of modulus, and cmod is the % operator from the C library. It also provides gcd (greatest common divisor) and lcm (least common multiple).

```
div I0, 12, 5  # I0 = 12 / 5
mod I0, 12, 5  # I0 = 12 % 5
```

Floating-point operations

Although most of the math operations work with both floating-point numbers and integers, a few require floating-point destination registers. Among these are ln (natural log), log2 (log base 2), log10 (log base 10), and exp (e^x), as well as a full set of trigonometric opcodes such as sin (sine), cos (cosine), tan (tangent), sec (secant), cosh (hyperbolic cosine), tanh (hyperbolic tangent), sech (hyperbolic secant), asin (arc sine), acos (arc cosine), atan (arc tangent), asec (arc secant), exsec (exsecant), hav (haversine), and vers (versine). All angle arguments for the trigonometric functions are in radians:

```
sin N1, N0
exp N1, 2
```

The majority of the floating-point operations have a single source argument and a single destination argument. Even though the destination must be a floating-point register, the source can be either an integer or floating-point number.

The atan opcode also has a three-argument variant that implements C's atan2( ):

```
atan N0, 1, 1
```

Working with Strings

The string operations work with string registers and with PMCs that implement a string class.

At the moment, operations on string registers generate new strings in the destination register. There are plans for an optimized set of string functions that modify an existing string in place. These might be implemented by the time you read this.

String operations on PMC registers require all their string arguments to be PMCs.

Concatenating strings

Use the concat opcode to concatenate strings. With string register or string constant arguments, concat has both a two-argument and a three-argument form. The first argument is a source and a destination in the two-argument form:

```
set S0, "ab"
concat S0, "cd"     # S0 has "cd" appended
print S0            # prints "abcd"
print "\n"

concat S1, S0, "xy" # S1 is the string S0 with "xy" appended
print S1            # prints "abcdxy"
print "\n"
end
```

The first concat concatenates the string "cd" onto the string "ab" in S0. It generates a new string "abcd" and changes S0 to point to the new string. The second concat concatenates "xy" onto the string "abcd" in S0 and stores the new string in S1.

For PMC registers, concat has only a three-argument form with separate registers for source and destination:

```
new P0, .PerlString
new P1, .PerlString
new P2, .PerlString
set P0, "ab"
set P1, "cd"
concat P2, P0, P1
print P2            # prints abcd
print "\n"
end
```

Here, concat concatenates the strings in P0 and P1 and stores the result in P2.

Repeating strings

The repeat opcode repeats a string a certain number of times:

```
set S0, "x"
repeat S1, S0, 5    # S1 = S0 x 5
print S1            # prints "xxxxx"
print "\n"
end
```

In this example, repeat generates a new string with "x" repeated five times and stores a pointer to it in S1.

Length of a string

The length opcode returns the length of a string in characters. This won't be the same as the length in bytes for multibyte encoded strings:

```
set S0, "abcd"
length I0, S0               # the length is 4
print I0
print "\n"
end
```

Currently, length doesn't have an equivalent for PMC strings, but it probably will be implemented in the future.

Substrings

The simplest version of the substr opcode takes four arguments: a destination register, a string, an offset position, and a length. It returns a substring of the original string, starting from the offset position (0 is the first character) and spanning the length:

```
substr S0, "abcde", 1, 2      # S0 is "bc"
```

This example extracts a string from "abcde" at a one-character offset from the beginning of the string (the second character) and spanning two characters. It generates a new string, "bc", in the destination register S0.

When the offset position is negative, it counts backward from the end of the string. So an offset of −1 starts at the last character of the string.

substr also has a five-argument form, where the fifth argument is a string to replace the substring. This modifies the second argument and returns the removed substring in the destination register.

```
set S1, "abcde"
substr S0, S1, 1, 2, "XYZ"
print S0                    # prints "bc"
print "\n"
print S1                    # prints "aXYZde"
```

```
print "\n"
end
```

This replaces the substring "bc" in S1 with the string "XYZ", and returns "bc" in S0.

When the offset position in a replacing substr is one character beyond the original string length, substr appends the replacement string just like the concat opcode.

When you don't need the replaced string, there's an optimized version of substr that just does a replace without returning the removed substring.

```
set S1, "abcde"
substr S1, 1, 2, "XYZ"
print S1                    # prints "aXYZde"
print "\n"
end
```

The PMC versions of substr are not yet implemented.

Chopping strings

The chopn opcode removes characters from the end of the string. It takes two arguments: the string to modify and the count of characters to remove. For example:

```
set S0, "abcde"
chopn S0, 2
print S0          # prints "abc"
print "\n"
end
```

removes two characters from the end of S0. If the count is negative, that many characters are kept in the string:

```
set S0, "abcde"
chopn S0, -2
print S0          # prints "ab"
print "\n"
end
```

This keeps the first two characters in S0 and removes the rest. chopn also has a three-argument version that stores the chopped string in a separate destination register, leaving the original string untouched:

```
set S0, "abcde"
chopn S1, S0, 1
print S1          # prints "abcd"
print "\n"
end
```

Copying strings

The clone opcode makes a deep copy of a string or PMC. Instead of just copying the pointer, as normal assignment would, it recursively copies the string or object underneath.

```
new P0, .PerlString
set P0, "Ford"
clone P1, P0
set P0, "Zaphod"
print P1        # prints "Ford"
end
```

This example creates an identical, independent clone of the PMC in P0 and puts a pointer to it in P1. Later changes to P0 have no effect on P1.

With simple strings, the copy created by clone, as well as the results from substr, are copy-on-write (COW). These are rather cheap in terms of memory usage because the new memory location is only created when the copy is assigned a new value. Cloning is rarely needed with ordinary string registers since they always create a new memory location on assignment.

Converting characters

The chr opcode takes an integer value and returns the corresponding character as a one-character string, while the ord opcode takes a single character string and returns the corresponding integer:

```
chr S0, 65         # S0 is "A"
ord I0, S0         # I0 is 65
```

ord has a three-argument variant that takes a character offset to select a single character from a multicharacter string. The offset must be within the length of the string:

```
ord I0, "ABC", 2     # I0 is 67
```

A negative offset counts backward from the end of the string, so −1 is the last character.

```
ord I0, "ABC", -1     # I0 is 67
```

Formatting strings

The sprintf opcode generates a formatted string from a series of values. It takes three arguments: the destination register, a string specifying the format, and an ordered aggregate PMC (like a PerlArray) containing the values to be formatted. The format string and the destination register can be either strings or PMCs:

```
sprintf S0, S1, P2
sprintf P0, P1, P2
```

The format string is similar to the one for C's sprintf function, but with some extensions for Parrot data types. Each format field in the string starts with a % and ends with a character specifying the output format. The output format characters are listed in Table 6-1.

Table 6-1. *Format characters*

Format	Meaning
%c	A character.
%d	A decimal integer.
%i	A decimal integer.
%u	An unsigned integer.
%o	An octal integer.
%x	A hex integer.
%X	A hex integer with a capital X (when # is specified).
%b	A binary integer.
%B	A binary integer with a capital B (when # is specified).
%p	A pointer address in hex.
%f	A floating-point number.
%e	A floating-point number in scientific notation (displayed with a lowercase "e").
%E	The same as %e, but displayed with an uppercase E.
%g	The same as either %e or %f, whichever fits best.
%G	The same as %g, but displayed with an uppercase E.
%s	A string.

Each format field can be specified with several options: *flags*, *width*, *precision*, and *size*. The format flags are listed in Table 6-2.

Table 6-2. *Format flags*

Flag	Meaning
0	Pad with zeros.
<space>	Pad with spaces.
+	Prefix numbers with a sign.
-	Align left.
#	Prefix a leading 0 for octal, 0x for hex, or force a decimal point.

The *width* is a number defining the minimum width of the output from a field. The *precision* is the maximum width for strings or integers, and the number of decimal places for floating-point fields. If either *width* or *precision* is an asterisk (*), it takes its value from the next argument in the PMC.

The *size* modifier defines the type of the argument the field takes. The flags are listed in Table 6-3.

Table 6-3. Size flags

Character	Meaning
h	short or float
l	long
H	huge value (long long or long double)
v	INTVAL or FLOATVAL
O	opcode_t
P	PMC
S	string

The values in the aggregate PMC must have a type compatible with the specified *size*.

Here's a short illustration of string formats:

```
new P2, .PerlArray
new P1, .PerlNum
new P0, .PerlInt
set P0, 42
set P1, 10
push P2, P0
push P2, P1
sprintf S0, "int %#Px num %+2.3Pf\n", P2
print S0      # prints "int 0x2a num +10.000"
print "\n"
end
```

The first eight lines create a `PerlArray` with two elements: a `PerlInt` and a `PerlNum`. The format string of the `sprintf` has two format fields. The first, `%#Px`, takes a PMC argument from the aggregate (P) and formats it as a hexadecimal integer (x), with a leading 0x (#). The second format field, `%+2.3Pf`, takes a PMC argument (P) and formats it as a floating-point number (f), with a minimum of two whole digits and a maximum of three decimal places (2.3) and a leading sign (+).

The test files *t/op/string.t* and *t/src/sprintf.t* have many more examples of format strings.

Testing for substrings

The `index` opcode searches for a substring within a string. If it finds the substring, it returns the position where the substring was found as a character offset from the beginning of the string. If it fails to find the substring, it returns −1:

```
index I0, "Beeblebrox", "eb"
print I0                      # prints 2
print "\n"
index I0, "Beeblebrox", "Ford"
print I0                      # prints -1
print "\n"
end
```

index also has a four-argument version, where the fourth argument defines an offset position for starting the search:

```
index I0, "Beeblebrox", "eb", 3
print I0                      # prints 5
print "\n"
end
```

This finds the second "eb" in "Beeblebrox" instead of the first, because the search skips the first three characters in the string.

I/O Operations

The I/O subsystem has at least one set of significant revisions ahead, so you can expect this section to change. It's worth an introduction, though, because the basic set of opcodes is likely to stay the same, even if their arguments and underlying functionality change.

Open and close a file

The open opcode opens a file for access. It takes three arguments: a destination register, the name of the file, and a modestring. With a PMC destination, it returns a ParrotIO object on success and a PerlUndef object on failure. With an integer destination, it returns an integer file descriptor on success and −1 on failure:

```
open P0, "people.txt", "<"
open I0, "people.txt"
```

The modestring specifies whether the file is opened in read-only (<), write-only (>), read-write (+>), or append mode (>>). open takes a modestring argument only when it's creating a ParrotIO object, and not when it's creating a file descriptor.

The close opcode closes a ParrotIO object or a file descriptor:

```
close P0      # close a PIO
close I0      # close a descriptor
```

Output operations

We already saw the print opcode in several examples above. The one argument form prints a register or constant to stdout. It also has a two-argument form: the first argument is the file descriptor or ParrotIO object where the value is printed. The standard file descriptors are 0 for stdin, 1 for stdout, and 2 for stderr.

```
print 2, S0          # print to stderr
printerr S0          # the same
print P0, "xxx"      # print to PIO in P0
```

write is similar to print, but it only works with integer file descriptors:

```
write 2, S0          # write string to stderr
```

Reading from files

The read opcode reads a specified number of bytes from either stdin or a ParrotIO object:

```
read S0, I0          # read from stdin up to I0 bytes into S0
read S0, P0, I0      # read from the PIO in P0
```

readline is a variant of read that works with file descriptors. It reads a whole line at a time, terminated by the newline character:

```
readline S0, I0      # read a line from descriptor I0
```

The seek opcode sets the current file position on a ParrotIO object. It takes four arguments: a destination register, a ParrotIO object, an offset, and a flag specifying the origin point:

```
seek I0, P0, I1, I2
```

In this example, the position of P0 is set by an offset (I1) from an origin point (I2). 0 means the offset is from the start of the file, 1 means the offset is from the current position, and 2 means the offset is from the end of the file. The return value (in I0) is 0 when the position is successfully set and −1 when it fails. seek also has a five-argument form that seeks with a 64-bit offset, constructed from two 32-bit arguments.

Logical and Bitwise Operations

The logical opcodes evaluate the truth of their arguments. They're often used to make decisions on control flow. Logical operations are implemented for integers and PMCs.

The and opcode returns the second argument if it's false and the third argument if the second one is true:

```
and I0, 0, 1  # returns 0
and I0, 1, 2  # returns 2
```

The or opcode returns the second argument if it's true and the third argument if the second is false:

```
or I0, 1, 0  # returns 1
or I0, 0, 2  # returns 2

or P0, P1, P2
```

Both and and or are short-circuiting. If they can determine what value to return from the second argument, they'll never evaluate the third. This is significant only for PMCs, as they might have side effects on evaluation.

The xor opcode returns the second argument if it is the only true value, returns the third argument if it is the only true value, and returns false if both values are true or both are false:

```
xor I0, 1, 0  # returns 1
xor I0, 0, 1  # returns 1
xor I0, 1, 1  # returns 0
xor I0, 0, 0  # returns 0
```

The not opcode returns a true value when the second argument is false, and a false value if the second argument is true:

```
not I0, I1
not P0, P1
```

The bitwise opcodes operate on their values a single bit at a time. band, bor, and bxor return a value that is the logical AND, OR, or XOR of each bit in the source arguments. They each take a destination register and two source registers. They also have two-argument forms where the destination is also a source. bnot is the logical NOT of each bit in a single source argument.

```
bnot I0, I1
band P0, P1
bor I0, I1, I2
bxor P0, P1, I2
```

The logical and arithmetic shift operations shift their values by a specified number of bits:

```
shl  I0, I1, I2    # shift I1 left by count I2 giving I0
shr  I0, I1, I2    # arithmetic shift right
lsr  P0, P1, P2    # logical shift right
```

Working with PMCs

In most of the examples we've shown so far, PMCs just duplicate the functionality of integers, numbers, and strings. They wouldn't be terribly useful if that's all they did, though. PMCs offer several advanced features, each with its own set of operations.

Aggregates

PMCs can define complex types that hold multiple values. These are commonly called "aggregates." The most important feature added for aggregates is keyed access. Elements within an aggregate PMC can be stored and retrieved by a numeric or string key. PASM also offers a full set of operations for manipulating aggregate data types.

Since PASM is intended to implement Perl, the two most fully featured aggregates already in operation are arrays and hashes. Any aggregate defined for any language could take advantage of the features described here.

Arrays

The `PerlArray` PMC is an ordered aggregate with integer keys. The syntax for keyed access to a PMC puts the key in square brackets after the register name:

```
new P0, .PerlArray  # obtain a new array object
set P0, 2           # set its length
set P0[0], 10       # set first element to 10
set P0[1], I31      # set second element to I31
set I0, P0[0]       # get the first element
set I1, P0          # get array length
```

A key on the destination register of a set operation sets a value for that key in the aggregate. A key on the source register of a set returns the value for that key. If you set P0 without a key, you set the length of the array, not one of its values.* And if you set an integer to the value of a `PerlArray`, you get the length of the array.

Some other useful instructions for working with arrays are push, pop, shift, and unshift (you'll find them later in "Writing Tests").

Hashes

The `PerlHash` PMC is an unordered aggregate with string keys:

```
new P1, .PerlHash      # generate a new hash object
set P1["key"], 10      # set key and value
set I0, P1["key"]      # obtain value for key
set I1, P1             # number of entries in hash
```

---

* `PerlArray` is an autoextending array, so you never need to set its length. Other array types may require the length to be set explicitly.

The exists opcode tests whether a keyed value exists in an aggregate. It returns 1 if it finds the key in the aggregate, and returns 0 if it doesn't. It doesn't care if the value itself is true or false, only that the key has been set:

```
new P0, .PerlArray
set P0[0], 0
exists I0, P0[0]   # does a value exist at key 0?
print I0           # prints 1
print "\n"
end
```

The delete opcode is also useful for working with hashes: it removes a key/ value pair.

Data structures

Arrays and hashes can hold any data type, including other aggregates. Accessing elements deep within nested data structures is a common operation, so PASM provides a way to do it in a single instruction. Complex keys specify a series of nested data structures, with each individual key separated by a semicolon:

```
new P0, .PerlHash
new P1, .PerlArray
set P1[2], 42
set P0["answer"], P1
set I1, 2
set I0, P0["answer";I1]      # $i = %hash{"answer"}[2]
print I0
print "\n"
end
```

This example builds up a data structure of a hash containing an array. The complex key P0["answer";I1] retrieves an element of the array within the hash. You can also set a value using a complex key:

```
set P0["answer";0], 5   # %hash{"answer"}[0] = 5
```

The individual keys are integers or strings, or registers with integer or string values.

PMC Assignment

We mentioned before that set on two PMCs simply aliases them both to the same object, and that clone creates a complete duplicate object. But if you just want to assign the value of one PMC to another PMC, you need the assign opcode:

```
new P0, .PerlInt
new P1, .PerlInt
set P0, 42
set P2, P0
```

```
assign P1, P0      # note: P1 has to exist already
inc P0
print P0           # prints 43
print "\n"
print P1           # prints 42
print "\n"
print P2           # prints 43
print "\n"
end
```

This example creates two PerlInt PMCs: P0 and P1. It gives P0 a value of 42. It then uses set to give the same value to P2, but uses assign to give the value to P1. When P0 is incremented, P2 also changes, but P1 doesn't. The destination register for assign must have an existing object of the right type in it, since assign doesn't create a new object (as with clone) or reuse the source object (as with set).

Properties

PMCs can have additional values attached to them as "properties" of the PMC. What these properties do is entirely up to the language being implemented. Perl 6 uses them to store extra information about a variable: whether it's a constant, if it should always be interpreted as a true value, etc.

The setprop opcode sets the value of a named property on a PMC. It takes three arguments: the PMC to be set with a property, the name of the property, and a PMC containing the value of the property. The getprop opcode returns the value of a property. It also takes three arguments: the PMC to store the property's value, the name of the property, and the PMC to have a property value retrieved:

```
new P0, .PerlString
set P0, "Zaphod"
new P1, .PerlInt
set P1, 1
setprop P0, "constant", P1      # set a property on P0
getprop P3, "constant", P0      # retrieve a property on P0
print P3                        # prints 1
print "\n"
end
```

This example creates a PerlString object in P0, and a PerlInt object with the value 1 in P1. setprop sets a property named "constant" on the object in P0 and gives the property the value in P1.* getprop retrieves the value of the property "constant" on P0 and stores it in P3.

---

* The "constant" property is ignored by PASM, but is significant to the Perl 6 code running on top of it.

Properties are kept in a separate hash for each PMC. Property values are always PMCs, but only references to the actual PMCs. Trying to fetch the value of a property that doesn't exist returns a PerlUndef.

delprop deletes a property from a PMC. You can also return a complete hash of all properties on a PMC with prophash.

```
prophash P0, P1          # set P0 to the property hash of P1
delprop P1, "constant"   # delete property
```

Flow Control

Although it has many advanced features, at heart PASM is an assembly language. All flow control in PASM—as in most assembly languages—is done with branches and jumps.

Branch instructions transfer control to a relative offset from the current instruction. The rightmost argument to every branch opcode is a label, which the assembler converts to the integer value of the offset. You can also branch on a literal integer value, but there's rarely any need to do so. The simplest branch instruction is branch:

```
    branch L1                # branch 4
    print "skipped\n"
L1:
    print "after branch\n"
    end
```

This example unconditionally branches to the location of the label L1, skipping over the first print statement.

Jump instructions transfer control to an absolute address. The jump opcode doesn't calculate an address from a label, so it's used together with set_addr:

```
    et_addr I0, L1
    jump I0
    print "skipped\n"
    end
L1:
    print "after jump\n"
    end
```

The set_addr opcode takes a label or an integer offset and returns an absolute address.

You've probably noticed the end opcode as the last statement in many examples above. This terminates the execution of the current bytecode segment. Terminating the main bytecode segment (the first one) stops the interpreter. Without the end statement, execution just falls off the end of the segment, with a good chance of crashing the interpreter.

Conditional Branches

Unconditional jumps and branches aren't really enough for flow control. What you need to implement the control structures of high-level languages is the ability to select different actions based on a set of conditions. PASM has opcodes that conditionally branch based on the truth of a single value or the comparison of two values. The following example has if and unless conditional branches:

```
    set I0, 0
    if I0, TRUE
    unless I0, FALSE
    print "skipped\n"
    end
TRUE:
    print "shouldn't happen\n"
    end
FALSE:
    print "the value was false\n"
    end
```

if branches if its first argument is a true value, and unless branches if its first argument is a false value. In this case, the if doesn't branch because I0 is false, but the unless does branch. Numeric values are false if they are 0, and true otherwise. Strings are false if they are the empty string or a single character "0", and true otherwise. PMCs are true when their get_bool vtable method returns a nonzero value.

The comparison branching opcodes compare two values and branch if the stated relation holds true. These are eq (branch when equal), ne (when not equal), lt (when less than), gt (when greater than), le (when less than or equal), and ge (when greater than or equal). The two compared arguments must be the same register type:

```
    set I0, 4
    set I1, 4
    eq I0, I1, EQUAL
    print "skipped\n"
    end
EQUAL:
    print "the two values are equal\n"
    end
```

This compares two integers, I0 and I1, and branches if they are equal. Strings of different character sets or encodings are converted to Unicode before they're compared. PMCs have a cmp vtable method. This gets called on the left argument to perform the comparison of the two objects.

Iteration

PASM doesn't define high-level loop constructs. These are built up from a combination of conditional and unconditional branches. A *do-while* style loop can be constructed with a single conditional branch:

```
set I0, 0
set I1, 10
REDO:
  inc I0
  print I0
  print "\n"
  lt I0, I1, REDO
  end
```

This example prints out the numbers 1 to 10. The first time through, it executes all statements up to the lt statement. If the condition evaluates as true (I0 is less than I1) it branches to the REDO label and runs the three statements in the loop body again. The loop ends when the condition evaluates as false.

Conditional and unconditional branches can build up quite complex looping constructs, as follows:

```
# loop ($i=1; $i<=10; $i++) {
#     print "$i\n";
# }
loop_init:
  set I0, 1
  branch loop_test
loop_body:
  print I0
  print "\n"
  branch loop_continue
loop_test:
  le I0, 10, loop_body
  branch out
loop_continue:
  inc I0
  branch loop_test
out:
  end
```

This example emulates a counter-controlled loop like Perl 6's loop keyword or C's for. The first time through the loop it sets the initial value of the counter in loop_init, tests that the loop condition is met in loop_test, and then executes the body of the loop in loop_body. If the test fails on the first iteration, the loop body will never execute. The end of loop_body branches to loop_continue, which increments the counter and then goes to loop_test again. The loop ends when the condition fails, and it branches to out. The example is more complex than it needs to be just to count to 10, but it nicely shows the major components of a loop.

Stacks and Register Frames

Parrot provides 32 registers of each type: integer, floating-point number, string, and PMC. This is a generous number of registers, but it's still too restrictive for the average use. You can hardly limit your code to 32 integers at a time. This is especially true when you start working with subroutines and need a way to store the caller's values and the subroutine's values. So, Parrot also provides stacks for storing values outside the 32 registers. Parrot has seven basic stacks, each used for a different purpose: the user stack, the control stack, the integer stack, and the four register backing stacks.*

User Stack

The user stack, also known as the general-purpose stack, stores individual values. The two main opcodes for working with the user stack are save, to push a value onto the stack, and restore, to pop one off the stack:

```
save 42       # push onto user stack
restore I1    # pop off user stack
```

The one argument to save can be either a constant or a register. The user stack is a typed stack, so restore will only pop a value into a register of the same type as the original value:

```
save 1
set I0, 4
restore I0
print I0      # prints 1
end
```

If that restore were restore N0 instead of an integer register, you'd get an exception, "Wrong type on top of stack!"

A handful of other instructions are useful for manipulating the user stack. rotate_up rotates a given number of elements on the user stack to put a different element on the top of the stack. The depth opcode returns the number of entries currently on the stack. The entrytype opcode returns the type of the stack entry at a given depth, and lookback returns the value of an element at the given depth without popping the element off the stack:

```
save 1
save 2.3
set S0, "hi\n"
save S0
save P0
```

---

* It also has a pad stack, which we'll discuss in "Lexicals and Globals."

```
entrytype I0, 0
print I0          # prints 4 (PMC)
entrytype I0, 1
print I0          # prints 3 (STRING)
entrytype I0, 2
print I0          # prints 2 (FLOATVAL)
entrytype I0, 3
print I0          # prints 1 (INTVAL)
print "\n"
depth I2          # get entries
print I2          # prints 4
print "\n"
lookback S1, 1    # get entry at depth 1
print S1          # prints "hi\n"
depth I2          # unchanged
print I2          # prints 4
print "\n"
end
```

This example pushes four elements onto the user stack: an integer, a floating-point number, a string, and a PMC. It checks the entrytype of all four elements and prints them out. It then checks the depth of the stack, gets the value of the second element with a lookback, and checks that the number of elements hasn't changed.

Control Stack

The control stack, also known as the call stack, stores the addresses for returning from subroutine calls. There are no instructions for directly manipulating the control stack, only calls to subroutines and returns from them. These opcodes are described in "Subroutines" later in this chapter.

Integer Stack

The integer stack, also known as the high-speed intstack, is a stack for storing integers. It's much faster than the general-purpose stack, because its operations are streamlined for a single, simple data type. The integer stack opcodes are intsave to push a value onto the integer stack, intrestore to pop a value off, and intdepth to get the current depth of the integer stack.

Register Frames

The final set of stacks are the register backing stacks. Instead of saving and restoring individual values, they work with register frames. Each register frame is the full set of 32 registers for one type. Parrot has four backing stacks, one for each type of register. The backing stacks are commonly used for saving the contents of all the registers before a subroutine call, so they can be restored when control returns to the caller.

PASM has five opcodes for storing register frames, one for each register type and one that saves all four at once:

```
pushi       # copy I-register frame
pushn       # copy N-register frame
pushs       # copy S-register frame
pushp       # copy P-register frame
saveall     # copy all register frames
```

Each pushi, pushn, pushs, or pushp pushes a register frame containing all the current values of one register type onto the backing stack of that type. saveall simply calls pushi, pushn, pushs, and pushp.

There are also five opcodes to restore register frames:

```
popi        # restore I-register frame
popn        # restore N-register frame
pops        # restore S-register frame
popp        # restore P-register frame
restoreall  # restore all register frames
```

The popi, popn, pops, and popp opcodes pop a single register frame off a particular stack and replace the values in all 32 registers of that type with the values in the restored register frame. restoreall calls popi, popn, pops, and popp, restoring every register of every type to values saved earlier.

Saving a register frame to the backing stack doesn't alter the values stored in the registers; it simply copies the values:

```
set I0, 1
print I0      # prints 1
pushi         # copy away I0..I31
print I0      # unchanged, still 1
inc I0
print I0      # now 2
popi          # restore registers to state of previous pushi
print I0      # old value restored, now 1
print "\n"
end
```

This example sets the value of I0 to 1 and stores the complete set of integer registers. Before I0 is incremented, it has the same value as before the pushi.

PASM also has opcodes to clear a register frame called cleari, clearn, clears, and clearp. These reset the numeric registers to 0 values and the string and PMC registers to null pointers, which is the same state they have when the interpreter first starts.

The user stack can be useful for holding onto some values that would otherwise be obliterated by a restoreall:

```
# ... coming from a subroutine
save I5      # Push some registers
save I6      # holding the return values
save N5      # of the sub.
restoreall  # restore registers to state before calling subroutine
restore N0  # pop off last pushed
restore I0  # pop 2nd
restore I1  # and so on
```

Lexicals and Globals

So far, we've been treating Parrot registers like the variables of a high-level language. This is fine, as far as it goes, but it isn't the full picture. The dynamic nature and introspective features of languages like Perl make it desirable to manipulate variables by name, instead of just by register or stack location. These languages also have global variables, which are visible throughout the entire program. Storing a global variable in a register would either tie up that register for the life of the program or require unwieldy manipulation of the user stack.

Parrot provides structures for storing both global and lexically scoped named variables. Lexical and global variables must be PMC values. PASM provides instructions for storing and retrieving variables from these structures so the PASM opcodes can operate on their values.

Globals

Global variables are stored in a PerlHash, so every variable name must be unique. PASM has two opcodes for globals, store_global and find_global:

```
new P10, .PerlInt
set P10, 42
store_global "$foo", P10
# ...
find_global P0, "$foo"
print P0                      # prints 42
end
```

The first two statements create a PerlInt in the PMC register P10 and give it the value 42.

The store_global opcode only stores a reference to the object. If we add an increment statement:

```
inc P10
```

after the store_global it increments the stored global printing 43. If that's not what you want, you can clone the PMC before you store it. It does have advantages, though. If you retrieve a stored global into a register and modify it as follows:

```
find_global P0, "varname"
inc P0
```

the value of the stored global is directly modified, so you don't need to call store_global again.

Lexicals

Lexical variables are stored in a lexical scratchpad. There's one pad for each lexical scope. Every pad has both a hash and an array, so elements can be stored either by name or by numeric index. Parrot stores the scratchpads for nested lexical scopes in a pad stack.

Basic instructions

The instructions for manipulating lexical scratchpads are new_pad to create a new pad, store_lex to store a variable in a pad, find_lex to retrieve a variable from a pad, push_pad to push a pad onto the pad stack, and pop_pad to remove a pad from the stack:

```
new_pad 0                 # create and push a pad with depth 0
new P0, .PerlInt          # create a variable
set P0, 10                # assign value to it
store_lex 0, "$foo", P0   # store the var at depth 0 by name
# ...
find_lex P1, 0, "$foo"    # get the var into P1
print P1
print "\n"                # prints 10
pop_pad                   # remove pad
end
```

The first statement creates a new scratchpad and pushes it onto the pad stack. It's created with depth 0, which is the outermost lexical scope. The next two statements create a new PMC object in P0, and give it a value. The store_lex opcode stores the object in P0 as the named variable $foo in the scratchpad at depth 0. At some later point in the program, the find_lex opcode retrieves the value of $foo in the pad at depth 0 and stores it in the register P1 so it can be printed. At the very end, pop_pad removes the pad from the pad stack.

The new_pad opcode has two forms, one that creates a new scratchpad and stores it in a PMC, and another that creates a new scratchpad and immediately pushes it onto the pad stack. If the pad were stored in a PMC, you would have to push it onto the pad stack before you could use it:

```
new_pad P10, 0          # create a new pad in P10
push_pad P10            # push it onto the pad stack
```

In a simple case like this, it really doesn't make sense to separate out the two instructions, but you'll see later in "Subroutines" why it's valuable to have both.

The store_lex and find_lex opcodes can take an integer index in place of a name for the variable:

```
store_lex 0, 0, P0  # store by index
# ...
find_lex P1, 0      # retrieve by index
```

With an index, the variable is stored in the scratchpad array, instead of the scratchpad hash.

Nested scratchpads

To create a nested scope, you create another scratchpad with a higher depth number and push it onto the pad stack. The outermost scope is always depth 0, and each nested scope is one higher. The pad stack won't allow you to push on a scratchpad that's more than one level higher than the current depth of the top of the stack:

```
new_pad 0                   # outer scope
new_pad 1                   # inner scope
new P0, .PerlInt
set P0, 10
store_lex -1, "$foo", P0    # store in top pad
new P1, .PerlInt
set P1, 20
store_lex -2, "$foo", P1    # store in next outer scope
find_lex P2, "$foo"         # find in all scopes
print P2                    # prints 10
print "\n"
find_lex P2, -1, "$foo"     # find in top pad
print P2                    # prints 10
print "\n"
find_lex P2, -2, "$foo"     # find in next outer scope
print P2                    # prints 20
print "\n"
pop_pad
pop_pad
end
```

The first two statements create two new scratchpads, one at depth 0 and one at depth 1, and push them onto the pad stack. When store_lex and find_lex have a negative number for the depth specifier, they count backward from the top pad on the stack. −1 is the top pad, and −2 is the second pad back. In this case, the pad at depth 1 is the top pad, and the pad at depth 0 is the second pad. So:

```
store_lex -1, "$foo", P0    # store in top pad
```

stores the object in P0 as the named variable $foo in the pad at depth 1. Then:

```
store_lex -2, "$foo", P1    # store in next outer scope
```

stores the object in P1 as the named variable $foo in the pad at depth 0.

A find_lex statement with no depth specified searches every scratchpad in the stack from the top of the stack to the bottom:

```
find_lex P2, "$foo"        # find in all scopes
```

Both pad 0 and pad 1 have variables named $foo, but only the value from the top pad is returned. store_lex also has a version with no depth specified, but it only works if the named lexical has already been created at a particular depth. It searches the stack from top to bottom and stores the object in the first lexical it finds with the right name.

The peek_pad instruction retrieves the top entry on the pad stack into a PMC register, but doesn't pop it off the stack.

Subroutines

Subroutines and methods are the basic building blocks of larger programs. At the heart of every subroutine call are two fundamental actions: it has to store the current location so it can come back to it, and it has to transfer control to the subroutine. The bsr opcode does both. It pushes the address of the next instruction onto the control stack, and then branches to a label that marks the subroutine:

```
    print "in main\n"
    bsr _sub
    print "and back\n"
    end
_sub:
    print "in sub\n"
    ret
```

At the end of the subroutine, the ret instruction pops a location back off the control stack and goes there, returning control to the caller. The jsr opcode pushes the current location onto the call stack and jumps to a subroutine. Just like the jump opcode, it takes an absolute address in an integer register, so the address has to be calculated first with the set_addr opcode:

```
print "in main\n"
set_addr I0, _sub
jsr I0
print "and back\n"
end
_sub:
print "in sub\n"
ret
```

Calling Conventions

A bsr or jsr is fine for a simple subroutine call, but few subroutines are
quite that simple. The biggest issues revolve around register usage. Parrot
has 32 registers of each type, and the caller and the subroutine share the
same set of registers. How does the subroutine keep from destroying the
caller's values? More importantly, who is responsible for saving and restoring registers? Where are arguments for the subroutine stored? Where are the
subroutine's return values stored? A number of different answers are possible. You've seen how many ways Parrot has of storing values. The critical
point is that the caller and the called subroutine have to agree on all the
answers.

Reserved registers

A very simple system would be to declare that the caller uses registers 0
through 15, and the subroutine uses 16 through 31. This works in a small
program with light register usage. But what about a subroutine call from
within another subroutine or a recursive call? The solution doesn't extend to
a large scale.

Callee saves

Another possibility is to make the subroutine responsible for saving the
caller's registers:

```
set I0, 42
save I0              # pass args on stack
bsr _inc             # j = inc(i)
restore I1           # restore args from stack
print I1
print "\n"
end
_inc:
saveall             # preserve all registers
restore I0          # get argument
inc I0              # do all the work
save I0             # push return value
restoreall          # restore caller's registers
ret
```

This example stores arguments to the subroutine and return values from the subroutine on the user stack. The first statement in the _inc subroutine is a saveall to save all the caller's registers onto the backing stacks, and the last statement before the return restores them.

One advantage of this approach is that the subroutine can choose to save and restore only the register frames it actually uses, for a small speed gain. The example above could use pushi and popi instead of saveall and restoreall because it only uses integer registers. One disadvantage is that it doesn't allow optimization of tail calls, where the last statement of a recursive subroutine is the call to itself.

Parrot calling conventions

Internal subroutines can use whatever calling convention serves them best. Externally visible subroutines and methods need stricter rules, since they might be called from a variety of contexts, even from multiple different high-level languages.

Under the Parrot calling conventions,* the caller is responsible for preserving its own registers. The first 11 arguments of each register type are passed in Parrot registers, as are several other pieces of information. Register usage for subroutine calls is listed in Table 6-4.

Table 6-4. Calling conventions

Register	Usage
P0	Subroutine object.
P1	Continuation if applicable.
P2	Object for a method call.
P3	Array with overflow parameters.
S0	Fully qualified subroutine name.
I0	True for prototyped parameters.
I1	Number of overflow arguments.
I3	Expected return type.
I5 ... I15	First 11 integer arguments.
N5 ... N15	First 11 float arguments.
S5 ... S15	First 11 string arguments.
P5 ... P15	First 11 PMC arguments.

* These conventions are still open to changes, so you'll want to check for the latest details in Parrot Design Document 3 (pdd03), available at *http://dev.perl.org/perl6/pdd/* and in *docs/pdds/pdd03_calling_conventions.pod.*

If there are more than 11 arguments of one type for the subroutine, over-flow parameters are passed in an array in P3. Subroutines without a proto-type pass all their arguments in the user stack or overflow array.*

Return values and additional information about them are also passed in reg-isters. The individual registers used on return are listed in Table 6-5.

Table 6-5. Return conventions

Register	Usage
I0	Registers on the stack.
I1	Number of integer return results.
I2	Number of string return results.
I3	Number of PMC return results.
I4	Number of float return results.
P3	Array with overflow return values.
I5 ... I15	First 11 integer return values.
N5 ... N15	First 11 float return values.
S5 ... S15	First 11 string return values.
P5 ... P15	First 11 PMC return values.

Overflow return values and return values from a subroutine without a proto-type are passed in the overflow array, just like subroutine arguments.

The _inc subroutine from above can be rewritten as a prototyped sub-routine:

```
    set I0, 42
    new P0, .Sub        # create a new Sub object
    set_addr I1, _inc   # get address of function
    set P0, I1          # and set it on the Sub object
    set I5, I0          # first integer argument
    set I0, 1           # prototype used
    saveall             # preserve environment
    invoke              # call function object in P0
    save I5             # save return value
    restoreall          # restore registers
    restore I1          # restore return value from stack
    print I1
    print "\n"
    end
_inc:
    inc I5              # do all the work
    ret
```

---

* Prototyped subroutines have a defined signature.

Instead of using a simple bsr, this set of conventions uses a subroutine object. There are several kinds of subroutine-like objects, but Sub is a class for PASM subroutines. The location of the subroutine is set in the Sub object by the absolute address of the subroutine's label.

Subroutine objects of all kinds can be called with the invoke opcode. With no arguments, it calls the subroutine in P0, which is the standard for the Parrot calling conventions. There is also an invoke Px instruction for calling objects held in a different register.

Native Call Interface

A special version of the Parrot calling conventions are used by the Native Call Interface (NCI) for calling subroutines with a known prototype in shared libraries. This is not really portable across all libraries, but it's worth a short example. This is the first of some tests in *t/pmc/nci.t*:

```
loadlib P1, "libnci.so"     # get library object for a shared lib
print "loaded\n"
dlfunc P0, P1, "nci_dd", "dd" # obtain the function object
print "dlfunced\n"
set I0, 1                   # prototype used - unchecked
set I1, 0                   # items on stack - unchecked
set N5, 4.0                 # first argument
saveall                     # preserve regs
invoke                      # call nci_dd
save N5                     # save return result
restoreall                  # restore registers
restore N5
ne N5, 8.0, nok_1           # the test functions returns 2*arg
print "ok 1\n"
end
nok_1:
    ...
```

This shows two new instructions: loadlib obtains a handle for a shared library, and dlfunc gets a function object from a loaded library (second argument) of a specified name (third argument) with a known function signature (fourth argument). The function signature is a string where the first character is the return value and the rest of the parameters are the function parameters. The characters used in NCI function signatures are listed in Table 6-6.

Table 6-6. Function signature letters

Character	Register set	C type
v	-	void (no return value)
c	I	char
s	I	short

Table 6-6. Function signature letters (continued)

Character	Register set	C type
i	I	int
l	I	long
f	N	float
d	N	double
t	S	char *
p	P	void * (or other pointer)
I	-	Parrot_Interp *interpreter

Closures

A closure is a subroutine that keeps values from the lexical scope where it was defined, even when it's called from an entirely different scope. The closure shown here is equivalent to this Perl 5 code snippet:

```
#    sub foo {
#        my ($n) = @_;
#        sub {$n += shift}
#    }
#    my $closure = foo(10);
#    print &$closure(3), "\n";
#    print &$closure(20), "\n";

# call _foo
new P0, .Sub            # new subroutine object
set_addr I3, _foo       # get address of _foo
set P0, I3              # attach address
new P5, .PerlInt        # define $n
set P5, 10
saveall                 # caller save
invoke                  # call foo
save P5                 # save return value
restoreall              # restore registers
restore P0              # get return value (the closure)

# call _closure
new P5, .PerlInt        # argument to closure
set P5, 3
saveall
invoke                  # call closure(3)
save P5                 # return value
restoreall
restore P2              # print result
print P2                # prints 13
print "\n"

# call _closure
set P5, 20              # and again
```

```
        saveall
        invoke                  # call closure(20)
        save P5
        restoreall
        restore P2
        print P2                # prints 33
        print "\n"
        end

_foo:
        new_pad 0               # push a new pad
        store_lex 0, "n", P5    # store $n
        new P5, .Sub            # P5 has the lexical "n" in the pad
        set_addr I3, _closure   # because the Sub inherits the lex pad
        set P5, I3              # set address of function
        pop_pad                 # cleanup
        ret                     # the Sub in P5 is the return value

_closure:
        find_lex P2, "n"        # invoking the Sub pushes the lexical pad
                                # of the closure on the pad stack
        add P2, P5              # n += shift
        set P5, P2              # set return value
        pop_pad                 # on each call, the lex pad is there
        ret                     # so pop it at end and return
```

That's quite a lot of PASM code for such a little bit of Perl 5 code, but anonymous subroutines and closures hide a lot of magic under that simple interface. The core of this example is that when the new subroutine is created in _foo with:

```
new P5, .Sub            # P5 has the lexical "n" in the pad
```

it inherits and stores the current lexical scratchpad—the topmost scratchpad on the pad stack at the time. Later, when _closure is invoked from the main body of code, the stored pad is automatically pushed onto the pad stack. So, all the lexical variables that were available when _closure was defined are available when it's called.

Coroutines

As we mentioned in the previous chapter, coroutines are subroutines that can suspend themselves and return control to the caller—and then pick up where they left off the next time they're called, as if they never left.

In PASM, coroutines are subroutine-like objects:

```
new P0, .Coroutine
```

The Coroutine object has its own user stack, context stack, and pad stack. The pad stack is inherited from the caller. When the coroutine invokes itself, it returns to the caller. The next time it's invoked, it continues to execute where it returned:

```
new_pad 0                # push a new lexical pad on stack
new P0, .PerlInt         # save one variable in it
set P0, 10
store_lex -1, "var", P0

new P0, .Coroutine       # make a new coroutine object
set_addr I0, _cor
set P0, I0               # set the address
saveall                  # preserve enivronment
invoke                   # invoke the coroutine
restoreall
print "back\n"
saveall
invoke                   # invoke coroutine again
restoreall
print "done\n"
pop_pad
end

_cor:
    find_lex P1, "var"   # inherited pad from caller
    print "in cor "
    print P1
    print "\n"
    inc P1               # var++
    invoke               # yield( )
    print "again "
    branch _cor          # next invocation of the coroutine
```

This prints out the result:

```
in cor 10
back
again in cor 11
done
```

The invoke inside the coroutine is commonly referred to as "yield." The coroutine never ends. When it reaches the bottom, it branches back up to _cor and executes until it hits invoke again.

Continuations

A continuation is a subroutine that gets a complete copy of the caller's context, including its own copy of the call stack. Invoking a continuation starts or restarts it at the entry point:

```
new P1, .PerlInt
set P1, 5

new P0, .Continuation
```

```
        set_addr I0, _con
        set P0, I0
_con:
        print "in cont "
        print P1
        print "\n"
        dec P1
        unless P1, done
        invoke                    # P0
done:
        print "done\n"
        end
```

This prints:

```
in cont 5
in cont 4
in cont 3
in cont 2
in cont 1
done
```

Evaluating a Code String

This isn't really a subroutine operation, but it does produce a code object
that can be invoked. In this case, it's a bytecode segment object.

The first step is to get an assembler or compiler for the target language:

```
compreg P1, "PASM1"
```

Within the Parrot interpreter the only language available is PASM1, which
compiles a single, fully qualified PASM instruction to bytecode:*

```
compile P0, P1, "set_i_ic I0, 10"
```

This places a bytecode segment object into the destination register P0, which
can then be invoked with invoke:

```
compreg P1, "PASM1"               # get compiler
set S1, "in eval\n"
compile P0, P1, "print_s S1"
invoke                            # eval code P0
print "back again\n"
end
```

Fully qualified opcode names include the types of their arguments in the
name: i is an integer register, ic is an integer constant, s is a string register,
sc is a string constant, n is a float register, nc is a float constant, and p is a
PMC register.

---

* IMCC also accepts PASM for PASM source files, and PIR for PIR source files.

Writing Tests

As we mentioned earlier, contributions to the Parrot project are welcome. Contributing tests is a good place to start. You don't have to understand the code behind a PASM opcode[*] to test it, you only have to understand what it's supposed to do. If you're working on some code and it doesn't do what the documentation advertises, you can isolate the problem in a test or series of tests and send them to the bug tracking system. There's a good chance the problem will be fixed before the next release. Writing tests makes it a lot easier for the developer to know when they've solved your problem—it's solved when your tests pass. It also prevents that problem from appearing again, because it's checked every time anyone runs make test. As you move along, you'll want to write tests for every bug you fix or new feature you add.

The Perl 5 testing framework is at the core of Parrot tests, particularly *Test:: Builder*. Parrot's *Parrot::Test* module is an interface to *Test::Builder* and implements the extra features needed for testing Parrot, like the fact that PASM code has to be compiled to bytecode before it runs.

The main Parrot tests are in the top-level *t/* directory of the Parrot source tree. *t/op* contains tests for basic opcodes and *t/pmc* has tests for PMCs. The names of the test files indicate the functionality tested, like *integer.t*, *number.t*, and *string.t*. Part of the *make test* target is the command *perl t/harness*, which runs all the .t files in the subdirectories under */t*. You can run individual test files by passing their names to the *harness* script:

```
$ perl t/harness t/op/string.t t/op/integer.t
```

Here's a simple example that tests the set opcode with integer registers, taken from *t/op/integer.t*:

```
output_is(<<CODE, <<OUTPUT, "set_i");
    set     I0, 42
    set     I1, I0
    print   I1
    print   "\\n"
    end
CODE
42
OUTPUT
```

The code here sets integer register I0 to the value 42, sets I1 to the value of I0, and then prints the value in I1. The test passes if the value printed was 42, and fails otherwise.

---

[*] Or IMCC instruction.

The output_is subroutine takes three strings: the code to run, the expected output, and a description of the test. The first two strings can be quite long, so the convention is to use Perl 5 here-documents. If you look into the code section, you'll see that the literal \n has to be escaped as \\n. Many tests use the non-interpolating (<<'CODE') form of here-document to avoid that problem. The description can be any text. In this case, it's the fully qualified name of the set opcode for integer registers, but it could have been "set a native integer register."

If you look up at the top of *integer.t*, you'll see the line:

```
use Parrot::Test tests => 38;
```

The use line for the *Parrot::Test* module imports a set of subroutines into the test file, including output_is. The end of the line gives the number of tests contained in the file.

The output_is subroutine looks for an exact match between the expected result and the actual output of the code. When the test result can't be compared exactly, you want output_like instead. It takes a Perl 5 regular expression for the expected output:

```
output_like(<<'CODE', <<'OUTPUT', "testing for text match");
...
CODE
/^Output is some \d+ number\n$/
OUTPUT
```

Parrot::Test also exports output_isnt, which tests that the actual output of the code *doesn't* match a particular value.

There are a few guidelines to follow when you're writing a test for a new opcode or checking that an existing opcode has full test coverage. Tests should cover the opcode's standard operation, corner cases, and illegal input. The first tests should always cover the basic functionality of an opcode. Further tests can cover more complex operations and the interactions between opcodes. If the test program is complex or obscure, it helps to add comments. Tests should be self-contained to make it easy to identify where and why a test is failing.

PASM Quick Reference

This is a condensed list of PASM opcodes, sorted alphabetically for easy reference. For complete details on each opcode and the latest changes, read docs/core_ops.pod, or look at all the .ops files in the main Parrot source directory. We've followed a few conventions. DEST is always the register where the result of the operation is stored. Sometimes the original value of

DEST is one of the source values. VAL indicates that the actual value might be a literal integer, float, or string, or a register containing an integer, float, string, or PMC. See core.ops for the combinations allowed with a particular operation.

abs

```
abs DEST
abs DEST, VAL
```

Return the absolute value of a number. If VAL is left out, DEST gets the absolute value of itself.

acos

```
acos DEST, VAL
```

The arc cosine of VAL in radians.

add

```
add DEST, VAL
add DEST, VAL, VAL
```

Add two values and return the sum. If only one VAL, add VAL to DEST.

and

```
and DEST, VAL1, VAL2
```

Logical AND. Return VAL1 if it's false, VAL2 if VAL1 is true.

asin

```
asin DEST, VAL
```

The arc sine of VAL in radians.

asec

```
asec DEST, VAL
```

The arc secant of VAL in radians.

assign

assign *DEST, VAL*

Assign a value to a PMC.

atan

atan *DEST, VAL*
atan *DEST, VAL1, VAL2*

The arc tangent of *VAL1* / *VAL2* in radians (sign significant). If no *VAL2*, the arc tangent of *VAL*.

band

band *DEST, VAL*
band *DEST, VAL, VAL*

Bitwise AND on two values. If only one *VAL*, bitwise AND on *DEST* and *VAL*.

bnot

bnot *DEST, VAL*

Bitwise NOT on *VAL*.

bor

bor *DEST, VAL, VAL*

Bitwise OR on two values. If only one *VAL*, bitwise OR on *DEST* and *VAL*.

bounds

bounds *INT*

Toggle bytecode bounds checking in the interpreter (0 for off, 1 for on).

branch

branch *LABEL*

Branch to a label. The label is calculated as a relative offset.

branch_cs

branch_cs *FIXUP_ENTRY*

Intersegment branch to the location of the given fixup table entry.

bsr

bsr *LABEL*

Branch to a label, like branch, but also push the current location onto the call stack so ret can return to it.

bxor

bxor *DEST, VAL*
bxor *DEST, VAL, VAL*

Bitwise XOR on two values. If only one *VAL*, bitwise XOR on *DEST* and *VAL*.

chopn

chopn *DEST, VAL1*
chopn *DEST, VAL1, VAL2*

Remove *VAL2* number of characters from string *VAL1*. If no *VAL2*, remove *VAL* number of characters from string *DEST*.

chr

chr *DEST, INT*

Return the character represented by the given number.

clearX

cleari
clearn
clearp
clears

Clear all registers of the given type ("i" = integer, "n" = float, "p" = PMC, "s" = string).

clone

clone *DEST, VAL*

Clone (deep copy) a string or PMC and return the result.

close

close *DEST*

Close the filehandle in the given register.

cmod

cmod *DEST, VAL1, VAL2*

C's built-in mod operator.

See also mod.

collect

collect

Trigger a garbage collection (GC) run.

collectoff

collectoff

Disable garbage collection runs (nestable).

collecton

collecton

Re-enable garbage collection runs.

compile

compile *DEST, COMPILER, SOURCE*

Compile a string of source code with a given compiler PMC and store the result.

compreg

compreg *DEST, TYPE*

Return a compiler PMC for a particular type of source code.

concat

concat *DEST, VAL*
concat *DEST, VAL, VAL*

Concatenate two strings. If only one *VAL*, concatenate *VAL* onto *DEST*.

cos

cos *DEST, VAL*

The cosine of *VAL* in radians.

cosh

cosh *DEST, VAL*

The hyperbolic cosine of *VAL* in radians.

debug

debug *INT*

Toggle debugging in the interpreter (0 for off, 1 for on).

dec

dec *DEST*

Decrement a value by 1.

defined

defined *DEST, PMC*
defined *DEST, PMC[KEY]*

Test a keyed PMC value for definedness. If no *KEY*, test a PMC for definedness.

delete

delete *DEST*[*KEY*]

Delete a keyed value from an aggregate PMC.

delprop

delprop *PMC, NAME*

Delete a named property from a PMC.

See also setprop and getprop.

depth

depth *DEST*

Return the depth of the user stack.

div

div *DEST, VAL*
div *DEST, VAL1, VAL2*

Divide *VAL1* by *VAL2*. If *VAL2* is left out, divide *DEST* by *VAL*.

dlfunc

dlfunc *DEST, LIBRARY, SYMBOL, SIGNATURE*

Look up a symbol in a dynamic link library PMC and create a subroutine PMC for that symbol with the given signature.

end

end

End execution within the current code segment or halt the interpreter if in the main code segment.

entrytype

entrytype *DEST, INT*

Return the type of an entry in the user stack, by position in the stack.

eq

eq *VAL, VAL, LABEL*

Jump to a label if the two values are equal.

err

err *DEST*

Return the system error code (INT) or message (STR).

exchange

exchange *REG, REG*

Exchange the contents of two registers.

exists

exists *DEST, PMC[KEY]*

Test a PMC key for existence.

exp

exp *DEST, VAL*

Base of the natural logarithm, *e*, to the power of *VAL*.

exsec

exsec *DEST, VAL*

The exsecant of *VAL* in radians.

fact

fact *DEST, INT*

Return the factorial of *INT*.

find_lex

```
find_lex DEST, NAME
find_lex DEST, DEPTH, NAME
find_lex DEST, DEPTH, POSITION
```

Return the lexical variable of the given name from a lexical scratchpad. If *DEPTH* is provided, only return a variable from the scratchpad at that depth. A find by position returns the variable at a particular position in the scratchpad.

See also store_lex.

find_global

```
find_global DEST, NAME
```

Return a global variable with the given name.

See also store_global.

find_method

```
find_method DEST, PMC, NAME
```

Look up a method by name in a PMC's vtable. Return a method PMC.

find_type

```
find_type DEST, NAME
```

Find the enum value for a PMC type or native Parrot datatype by name.

See also typeof.

getfile

```
getfile DEST
```

Return the name of the current file.

getline

```
getline DEST
```

Return the current line number.

getpackage

getpackage *DEST*

Return the current package name.

getprop

getprop *DEST, NAME, PMC*

Return the value of a named property on a PMC.

See also setprop and prophash.

gcd

gcd *DEST, VAL, VAL*

Return the greatest common divisor of two values.

gc_debug

gc_debug *INT*

Toggle garbage collection debugging in the interpreter (0 for off, 1 for on).

ge

ge *VAL1, VAL2, LABEL*

Jump to a label if *VAL1* is greater than or equal to *VAL2*.

gt

gt *VAL1, VAL2, LABEL*

Jump to a label if *VAL1* is greater than *VAL2*.

hav

hav *DEST, VAL*

The haversine of *VAL* in radians.

if

if *CONDITION, LABEL*

Jump to a label if the condition is a true value.

index

index *DEST, STRING, SEARCH*
index *DEST, STRING, SEARCH, POS*

Return the position of the first occurrence of *SEARCH* string in *STRING*, starting at *POS*. If the *POS* is unspecified, start at the beginning of the string.

inc

inc *DEST*

Increment a value by one.

intdepth

intdepth *DEST*

Return the depth of the integer stack.

interpinfo

interpinfo *DEST, FLAG*

Return information about the interpreter. An integer flag selects which information to return, as listed in Table 6-7.

Table 6-7. Interpinfo flags

Flag	Returns
1	Allocated memory, in bytes.
2	Number of DOD sweeps performed.
3	Number of GC runs performed.
4	Number of active PMCs.
5	Number of active buffers.
6	Number of allocated PMCs.
7	Number of allocated buffers.
8	Number of new PMC or buffer headers allocated since last DOD run.
9	Number of memory blocks allocated since last GC run.
10	Amount of memory copied during GC runs, in bytes.

intrestore

```
intrestore DEST
```

Restore a register from the integer stack.

intsave

```
intsave VAL
```

Save a value onto the integer stack.

invoke

```
invoke
invoke PMC
```

Call a subroutine, coroutine, or continuation stored in a PMC. If no PMC register is specified, it calls the subroutine in P0 and uses the standard calling conventions. Otherwise, no calling convention is defined. Also yield from a coroutine.

jump

```
jump ADDRESS
```

Jump to a specified absolute address.

See also set_addr.

jsr

```
jsr ADDRESS
```

Jump to an address, like jump, but also push the current location onto the call stack so ret can return to it.

lcm

```
lcm DEST, VAL, VAL
```

Return the least common multiple of two values.

le

```
le VAL1, VAL2, LABEL
```

Jump to a label if VAL1 is less than or equal to VAL2.

length

length *DEST, STRING*

Return the character length of a string.

ln

ln *DEST, VAL*

The natural logarithm of *VAL*.

loadlib

loadlib *DEST, LIBRARY*

Load a dynamic link library by name and store it in a PMC.
See also dlfunc.

log2

log2 *DEST, VAL*

The base 2 logarithm of *VAL*.

log10

log10 *DEST, VAL*

The base 10 logarithm of *VAL*.

lookback

lookback *DEST, OFFSET*

Retrieve an entry from the user stack by position. A positive offset counts from the top of the stack; a negative offset counts from the bottom.

lsr

lsr *DEST, VAL, BITS*

Logically shift a value right by a given number of bits.

lt

```
lt VAL1, VAL2, LABEL
```

Jump to a label if *VAL1* is less than *VAL2*.

mul

```
mul DEST, VAL
mul DEST, VAL, VAL
```

Multiply two values and return the result. If only one *VAL*, multiply *DEST* by *VAL*.

mod

```
mod DEST, VAL
mod DEST, VAL1, VAL2
```

Divide *VAL1* by *VAL2* and return the remainder. If *VAL2* is left off, divide *DEST* by *VAL*. The operation is defined as:

```
x mod y = x - y * floor(x / y)
```

ne

```
ne VAL, VAL, LABEL
```

Jump to a label if the two values are not equal.

neg

```
neg DEST
neg DEST, VAL
```

Return the negative of a number. If there is no *VAL*, *DEST* is the negative of itself.

new

```
new DEST, TYPE
new DEST, TYPE, INITIALIZE
```

Create a new PMC of type *TYPE*. *INITIALIZE* is an array PMC of initialization data for the new PMC.

new_pad

new_pad *DEPTH*
new_pad *DEST, DEPTH*

Create a new lexical scope pad. If a destination PMC is provided, store the pad in the PMC, otherwise push it onto the lexical scope stack. *DEPTH* specifies the static nesting depth for the pad (lower static depths are copied from the current static nesting).

newinterp

newinterp *DEST, FLAGS*

Create a new interpreter and store it in a PMC.

See also runinterp.

noop

noop

Do nothing.

not

not *DEST, VAL*

Logical NOT. True if *VAL* is false.

open

open *DEST, FILENAME, MODE*

Open a file in the specified mode ("<", ">", etc.) and return a filehandle.

or

or *DEST, VAL1, VAL2*

Logical OR. Return *VAL1* if it's true, *VAL2* if *VAL1* is false.

ord

ord *DEST, STRING*
ord *DEST, STRING, POS*

Return the character at position *POS* in *STRING*. If *POS* isn't specified, return the 0th character.

peek_pad

peek_pad *DEST*

Store the current lexical scope pad in a PMC.

pop

pop *DEST, PMC*

Pop the last entry off an aggregate PMC and return it.

pop_pad

pop_pad

Pop the current lexical scope pad off the lexical scope stack.

See also peek_pad.

popX

popi
popn
popp
pops

Restore all the registers of one type from the stack ("i" = integer, "n" = float, "p" = PMC, "s" = string).

See also pushX.

pow

pow *DEST, VAL1, VAL2*

Return *VAL1* raised to the power of *VAL2*.

print

```
print VAL
print IO, VAL
```

Print a value to an I/O object or file descriptor. If no *IO* is given, print the value to standard output.

printerr

```
printerr STR
```

Print a string to stderr.

profile

```
profile INT
```

Toggle profiling in the interpreter (0 for off, 1 for on).

prophash

```
prophash DEST, PMC
```

Return a hash containing all the properties from a PMC.

See also getprop.

push

```
push PMC, VAL
```

Push a value onto the end of an aggregate PMC.

push_pad

```
push_pad PAD
```

Push a scratchpad stored in a PMC onto the lexical scope stack.

pushX

```
pushi
pushn
pushp
pushs
```

Save all the registers of one type to the stack ("i" = integer, "n" = float, "p" = PMC, "s" = string). Restore with popX.

puts

puts *VAL*

Print a value to stdout.

read

read *DEST, BYTES*
read *DEST, IO, BYTES*

Read the specified number of bytes from a Parrot I/O object. Read from stdin if no *IO* is provided.

repeat

repeat *DEST, VAL, REPEAT*

Repeat a string *REPEAT* number of times.

restore

restore *DEST*

Restore a register from the user stack.

restoreall

restoreall

Restore all the registers. Does a pop*X* for every type.

ret

ret

Go to the location on the top of the call stack (also pop it off the stack). Often used with bsr and jsr.

rotate_up

rotate_up *COUNT*

Rotate the top *COUNT* entries on the user stack. A positive number rotates up: the top entry becomes the *COUNT*th entry, and the others move up one (the second entry becomes first, the third becomes the second, etc.). A negative number rotates down: the *COUNT*th entry becomes the top, and the others move down (the first becomes second, etc.).

runinterp

runinterp *PMC, OFFSET*

Use an interpreter stored in PMC to run code starting at a given offset.
See also newinterp.

save

save *VAL*

Save a value onto the user stack.

saveall

saveall

Save all the registers. Does a pushX for every type.

savec

savec *VAL*

Save a clone of a value onto the user stack.

sec

sec *DEST, VAL*

The secant of *VAL* in radians.

sech

sech *DEST, VAL*

The hyperbolic secant of *VAL* in radians.

seek

seek *DEST, IO, OFFSET, STARTFLAG*
seek *DEST, IO, UPPER32, LOWER32, STARTFLAG*

Set the file position of a Parrot I/O object to a given offset from a starting position (STARTFLAG: 0 is the beginning of the file, 1 is current the position, 2 is the end of the file). *DEST* is the success or failure of the seek.

64-bit seek combines *UPPER32* and *LOWER32* to get one 64-bit *OFFSET*.

set

`set DEST, VAL`

Set a register to a value.

`set DEST[KEY], VAL`

A keyed set operation on a PMC.

`set DEST, PMC[KEY]`

A keyed get operation on a PMC.

set_addr

`set_addr DEST, LABEL`

Return the current address plus the offset to `LABEL`. Often used to calculate absolute addresses for `jump` or `jsr`.

setprop

`setprop PMC, NAME, VALUE`

Set the value of a named property on a PMC.

See also getprop and delprop.

shift

`shift DEST, PMC`

Shift a value off the front of an aggregate PMC.

shl

`shl DEST, VAL, BITS`

Bitwise shift a value left by a given number of bits.

shr

`shr DEST, VAL, BITS`

Bitwise shift a value right by a given number of bits.

sin

sin *DEST, VAL*

The sine of *VAL* in radians.

sleep

sleep *SECONDS*

Sleep for the given number of seconds.

splice

splice *DEST, REPLACE, OFFSET, COUNT*

Starting at *OFFSET*, replace *COUNT* number of values in the destination PMC with values provided in the *REPLACE* PMC.

sprintf

sprintf *DEST, FORMAT, ARGS*

Format arguments in an aggregate PMC, using format string *FORMAT*.

store_lex

store_lex *NAME, OBJECT*
store_lex *DEPTH, NAME, OBJECT*
store_lex *DEPTH, POSITION, OBJECT*

Store an object as a lexical variable with a given name. If the symbol doesn't exist, it will be created in the lexical scratchpad at the specified depth (a negative depth counts back from the current scope). If *DEPTH* isn't provided, the symbol must already exist. If a position is provided instead of a name, the symbol will be stored at the given position in the scratchpad.

See also find_lex.

store_global

store_global *NAME, OBJECT*

Store a global variable as a named symbol.

See also find_global.

stringinfo

stringinfo *DEST, STRING, FLAG*

Return information about a string. An integer flag selects which information to return, as listed in Table 6-8.

Table 6-8. Stringinfo arguments

Flag	Returns
1	Location of string buffer header.
2	Location of start of string memory.
3	Allocated length, in bytes.
4	String flags.
5	Used length of string buffer, in bytes.
6	String length, in characters.

sub

sub *DEST, VAL*
sub *DEST, VAL1, VAL2*

Subtract *VAL2* from *VAL1*. If no *VAL2*, subtract *VAL* from *DEST*.

substr

substr *DEST, STRING, OFFSET, LENGTH*
substr *DEST, STRING, OFFSET, LENGTH, REPLACE*
substr *DEST, OFFSET, LENGTH, REPLACE*

Return a substring of a string. If *REPLACE* is given, also replace substring in *STRING*. If *STRING* is left out, replace substring in *DEST*.

sweep

sweep

Trigger a dead object detection (DOD) sweep.

sweepoff

sweepoff

Disable DOD sweeps (nestable).

sweepon

```
sweepon
```

Re-enable DOD sweeps.

tan

```
tan DEST, VAL
```

The tangent of VAL in radians.

tanh

```
tanh DEST, VAL
```

The hyperbolic tangent of VAL in radians.

time

```
time DEST
```

Return the current system time.

trace

```
trace INT
```

Toggle tracing in the interpreter (0 for off, 1 for on).

typeof

```
typeof DEST, VAL
```

Return the type of a PMC or Parrot data type, either class name (to a string destination) or enum value (to an integer destination).

unless

```
unless CONDITION, LABEL
```

Jump to a label unless the condition is a true value.

unshift

unshift *PMC*, *VAL*

Unshift a value onto the front of an aggregate PMC.

valid_type

valid_type *DEST*, *TYPE*

Check whether a PMC type or native Parrot datatype is a valid one.

vers

vers *DEST*, *VAL*

The versine of *VAL* in radians.

warningsoff

warningsoff *CATEGORY*

Turn off a particular category of warnings: 1 = undef, 2 = IO, −1 = all.

warningson

warningson *CATEGORY*

Turn on a particular category of warnings: 1 = undef, 2 = IO, −1 = all.

xor

xor *DEST*, *VAL1*, *VAL2*

Logical XOR. Return *VAL1* if it's true and *VAL2* is false. Return *VAL2* if *VAL2* is true and *VAL1* is false. Otherwise, return false.

CHAPTER 7

The Intermediate Code Compiler

Gentlemen, we can rebuild him. We have
the technology. [...] Better than he was
before. Better...stronger...faster.
—Oscar Goldman
  The Six Million Dollar Man

The Intermediate Code Compiler (IMCC) is an alternate tool for creating
and running Parrot bytecode. It has several advantages over the method
introduced in the previous chapter. It's a Parrot assembler and embeds the
Parrot runtime engine, so it can compile a PASM file to bytecode and immediately run the bytecode with a single command. IMCC can also perform
code optimizations, though it doesn't by default.

IMCC includes its own language, which is commonly called Parrot Intermediate Language (PIR). PIR is an overlay on top of Parrot assembly language
and has many higher-level features, though it still isn't a high-level language. Assembly files containing PIR code end with an *.imc* extension.

Getting Started

The first step to working with IMCC is to compile it. First, build Parrot following the steps in the previous chapter. Then, from within the *languages/
imcc* directory in the *parrot* repository, type:

```
$ make
$ make test
```

It's likely that by the time you read this, you won't have to compile IMCC at
all. One of the planned tasks is to include these steps in Parrot's *Makefile*, so
it will be done when you compile Parrot.

After compiling IMCC, create a file *fjords.pasm* in the *languages/imcc* directory with these two lines (or reuse the file from Chapter 6):

```
print "He's pining for the fjords.\n"
end
```

IMCC compiles and runs the code in a single step:

```
$ ./imcc fjords.pasm
```

It's a little more convenient than the separate assembler and interpreter we introduced in the last chapter.

If your system supports soft links, you might find it handy to have a symlink to *imcc* in Parrot's root directory, or a directory in your PATH. You can try out all the examples in this chapter by copying the code into a test file with the *.imc* extension. If *imcc* is in your path, run the examples as:

```
$ imcc example.imc
```

or with the -t option to trace the code as it executes:

```
$ imcc -t example.imc
```

Basics

IMCC's main purpose is assembling PASM or PIR source files. It can run them immediately or generate a Parrot bytecode file for running later.

Internally, IMCC works a little differently with PASM and PIR source code, so each has different restrictions. The default is to run in a "mixed" mode that allows PASM code to mix with the higher-level syntax unique to PIR.

A file with a *.pasm* extension is treated as pure PASM code, as is any file run with the -a command-line option. These files can use macros,* but none of PIR's syntax. This mode is mainly used for running pure PASM tests that were originally written for *assemble.pl*.

The documentation that comes with IMCC in *languages/imcc/docs/* and the test suite in *languages/imcc/t* are good starting points for digging deeper into its syntax and functionality.

---

* The only macro that works within PIR code is .include.

Statements

The syntax of statements in PIR is much more flexible than PASM. All PASM opcodes are valid PIR code, so the basic syntax is still an opcode followed by its arguments:

```
print "He's pining for the fjords.\n"
```

The statement delimiter is a newline \n, just like PASM, so each statement has to be on its own line. Any statement can start with a label.

```
LABEL: print I1
```

But unlike PASM, PIR has some higher-level constructs, including symbol operators:

```
I1 = 5
```

named variables:

```
count = 5
```

and complex statements built from multiple keywords and symbol operators:

```
if I1 <= 5 goto LABEL
```

We'll get into these in more detail as we go.

Comments

Comments are marked by a hash sign (#). Commented lines are counted but otherwise ignored, just like empty lines.

```
I1 = 5 # assign '5'
```

Variables and Constants

Constants in PIR are the same as constants in PASM. Integers and floating-point numbers are numeric literals:

```
print 42        # integer constant
print 0x2A      # hexadecimal integer
print 0b1101    # binary integer
print 3.14159   # floating point constant
print 1.e6      # scientific notation
```

Strings are enclosed in quotes:

```
print "fjord"
```

These can use the standard escape sequences, like \t (tab), \n (newline), \r (return), \f (form feed), \\ (literal slash), \" (literal double quote), etc. The

---

one difference from PASM strings is that in PIR strings the NULL character must be escaped as \x00:

```
print "Binary\x00nul embedded"
```

PASM registers

PIR code has a variety of ways to store values while you work with them. The most basic way is to use Parrot registers directly. Parrot register names always start with a single character that shows whether it is an integer, numeric, string, or PMC register, and end with the number of the register (between 0 and 31):

```
set S0, "Hello, Polly.\n"
print S0
end
```

This example is plain PASM syntax, but you can also use PASM registers in PIR code.

When you work directly with PASM registers, you can only have 32 registers of any one type at a time.* If you have more than that, you have to start shuffling stored values on and off the user stack. You also have to manually track when it's safe to reuse a register. This kind of low-level access to the Parrot registers is handy when you need it, but it's pretty unwieldy for large sections of code.

Temporary registers

IMCC provides an easier way to work with Parrot registers. The temporary register variables are named like the PASM registers—with a single character for the type of register and a number—but they start with a $ character:

```
set $S42, "Hello, Polly.\n"
print $S42
end
```

The most obvious difference between PASM registers and temporary register variables is that you have an unlimited number of temporaries. IMCC handles register allocation for you. It keeps track of how long a value in a Parrot register is needed and when that register can be reused.

The previous example used the $S42 temporary. When the code is compiled, that temporary is allocated to the Parrot register S0. As long as that

---

* Only 31 for PMC registers, because P31 is reserved for spilling.

temporary is needed, it is stored in S0. When it's no longer needed, S0 is re-allocated to some other value:

```
$S42 = "Hello, "
print $S42
$S43 = "Polly.\n"
print $S43
end
```

This example uses two temporary string registers. Since they don't overlap, both will be allocated to the S0 register. If you change the order a little so both temporaries are needed at the same time, they're allocated to different registers:

```
$S42 = "Hello, "  # allocated to S1
$S43 = "Polly.\n" # allocated to S0
print $S42
print $S43
end
```

In this case, $S42 is allocated to S1 and $S43 is allocated to S0.

IMCC allocates temporary registers* to Parrot registers in ascending order of their score. The score is based on a number of factors related to variable usage. Variables used in a loop have a higher score than variables outside a loop. Variables that span a long range have a lower score than ones that are used only briefly.

If you want to peek behind the curtain and see how IMCC is allocating registers, you can run it with the -d switch to turn on debugging output.

```
$ imcc -d1000 hello.imc
```

If *hello.imc* is the first example above, it produces this output:

```
code_size(ops) 11  oldsize 0
0 set_s_sc 0 1   set S0, "Hello, "
3 print_s 0      print S0
5 set_s_sc 0 0   set S0, "Polly.\n"
8 print_s 0      print S0
10 end   end
Hello, Polly.
```

That's probably a lot more information than you wanted if you're just starting out. You can also generate a PASM file with the -o switch and have a look at how the PIR code translates:

```
$ imcc -o hello.pasm hello.imc
```

---

* As well as named variables, which we'll talk about next.

You'll find more details on these options and many others in "IMCC Command-Line Options" later in this chapter.

Named variables

Named variables can be used anywhere a register or temporary register is used. They're declared with the `.local` statement or the equivalent `.sym` statement, which require a variable type and a name:

```
.local string hello
set hello, "Hello, Polly.\n"
print hello
end
```

This example defines a string variable named `hello`, assigns it the value "Hello, Polly.\n", and then prints the value.

The valid types are `string`, `int`, `float`, and any Parrot class name (like `PerlInt` or `PerlString`). It should come as no surprise that these are the same divisions as Parrot's four register types. IMCC allocates named variables to Parrot registers the same way it allocates temporary register variables.

The name of a variable must be a valid PIR identifier. It can contain letters, digits, and underscores, but the first character has to be a letter or underscore. Identifiers don't have any limit on length yet, but it's a safe bet they will before the production release.

Parrot classes

Any integer, floating-point number, or string can be replaced by an equivalent Parrot class:

```
P0 = new PerlString        # same as new P0, .PerlString
P0 = "Hello, Polly.\n"
print P0
end
```

Here, a `PerlString` object is created with the new *CLASSNAME* syntax[*] and stored in the PMC register P0. It gets assigned the string value "Hello, Polly.\n" and then printed. The syntax is exactly the same with temporary register variables:

```
$P4711 = new PerlString
$P4711 = "Hello, Polly.\n"
print $P4711
end
```

---

[*] Unlike PASM, IMCC doesn't use a dot in front of the class name.

With named variables the Parrot class has to be specified both as the type for the .local statement and as the class name for the new:

```
.local PerlString hello
hello = new PerlString
hello = "Hello, Polly.\n"
print hello
end
```

Another important instruction for working with Parrot classes is clone. A simple assignment of a Parrot class only creates an alias:

```
.local PerlString hello
hello = new PerlString
hello = "Hello, "
$P0 = hello              # PASM: set P0, P1
$P0 = "Polly.\n"
hello = hello . $P0
print hello
end
```

This prints:

```
Polly.
Polly.
```

In this example, $P0 and hello are really the same string. When you assign to one, you've assigned to both. To get a true copy, you have to use $P0 = clone hello instead of $P0 = hello, as follows:

```
.local PerlString hello
hello = new PerlString
hello = "Hello, "
$P0 = clone hello       # PASM: clone P0, P1
$P0 = "Polly.\n"
hello = hello . $P0
print hello
end
```

This prints:

```
Hello, Polly.
```

Named constants

Named constants are declared with a .const statement. It's very similar to .local, and requires a type and a name. The value must be assigned in the declaration statement:

```
.const string hello = "Hello, Polly.\n"
print hello
end
```

This example declares a named string constant hello and prints the value. Named constants can be used in all the same places as literal constants, but have to be declared beforehand:

```
.const int the_answer = 42      # integer constant
.const string mouse = "Mouse"   # string constant
.const float pi = 3.14159       # floating point constant
```

Register spilling

As we mentioned earlier, IMCC allocates Parrot registers for all temporary register variables and named variables. When IMCC runs out of registers to allocate, some of the variables have to be stored elsewhere. This is known as "spilling." IMCC spills the variables with the lowest score. It stores the spilled variable in a PerlArray object while it isn't used, then restores it to a register the next time it's needed:

```
set $I1, 1
set $I2, 2
...
set $I33, 33
...
print $I1
print $I2
...
print $I33
```

If you create 33 integer variables like this—all containing values that are used later—IMCC allocates the available integer registers to variables with a higher score and spills the variables with a lower score. In this example it picks $I1 and $I2. Behind the scenes, IMCC generates code to store the values:

```
new P31, .PerlArray
...
set I0, 1          # I0 allocated to $I1
set P31[0], I0     # spill $I1
set I0, 2          # I0 reallocated to $I2
set P31[1], I0     # spill $I2
```

It creates a PerlArray object and stores it in register P31.* The set instruction is the last time $I1 is used for a while, so immediately after that, IMCC stores its value in the spill array and frees up I0 to be reallocated.

Just before $I1 and $I2 are accessed to be printed, IMCC generates code to fetch the values from the spill array:

```
...
set I0, P31[0]     # fetch $I1
print I0
```

---

* P31 is reserved for register spilling in PIR code, so generally it shouldn't be accessed directly.

Symbol Operators

You probably noticed the = assignment operator in some of the earlier examples:

```
$S2000 = "Hello, Polly.\n"
print $S2000
end
```

Standing alone, it's the same as the PASM set opcode. In fact, if you run *imcc* in bytecode debugging mode (as in "Temporary registers"), you'll see it really is just a set opcode underneath.

PIR has many other symbol operators: arithmetic, concatenation, comparison, bitwise, and logical. Many of these combine with assignment to produce the equivalent of a PASM opcode:

```
.local int sum
sum = $I42 + 5
print sum
print "\n"
end
```

The statement sum = $I42 + 5 translates to add I0, I1, 5.

A complete list of operators is available in "IMCC Quick Reference." We'll discuss the comparison operators in "Flow Control."

Labels

A label names a line of code so other instructions can refer to it. Label names have to be valid PIR identifiers, just like named variables, so they're made of letters, numbers, and underscores. Simple labels are often all caps to make them stand out more clearly. A label definition is simply the name of the label followed by a colon. It can be on its own line:

```
LABEL:
    print "Norwegian Blue\n"
```

or before a statement on the same line:

```
LABEL: print "Norwegian Blue\n"
```

IMCC has both local and global labels. Global labels start with an underscore. The name of a global label has to be unique, since it can be called at any point in the program. Local labels start with a letter. A local label is accessible only in the compilation unit where it's defined.* The name has to be unique there, but it can be reused in a different compilation unit.

---

* We'll discuss compilation units in the next section.

```
branch L1   # local label
bsr    _L2  # global label
```

Labels are most often used in branching instructions and in calculating addresses for jumps.

Compilation Units

Compilation units in PIR are roughly equivalent to the subroutines or methods of a high-level language. They start with the .sub directive and end with the .end directive:

```
.sub _main
    print "Hello, Polly.\n"
    end
.end
```

This example defines a compilation unit named _main that prints a string. The name is actually a global label for this piece of code. If you generate a PASM file from the PIR code (see "Temporary registers"), you'll see that the name translates to an ordinary label:

```
_main:
        print "Hello, Polly.\n"
        end
```

The compilation units in a file and the code outside of compilation units are parsed and processed all at once. IMCC emits each compilation unit to byte-code or PASM code as a unit when it reaches the .end directive.

The first compilation unit in a file is special. The convention is to call it _main, but the name isn't critical. Since it's emitted first, it's always executed first. This means that when it closes with an end, nothing else in the file will ever execute unless it's called from within _main.

Any statements outside a compilation unit are emitted after all the compilation units. Generally this means such code is skipped:

```
print "Polly want a cracker?\n"

.sub _main
    print "Hello, Polly.\n"
    end
.end
```

This code prints out "Hello, Polly." but not "Polly want a cracker?" because end halts the interpreter, so it never reaches the statement outside the compilation unit.

Directives to IMCC (which start with a ".") aren't delayed like other statements. So, if you declare a named variable or named constant outside a compilation unit, it will be available to any statements that follow it:

```
.local string hello
hello = "Polly want a cracker?\n"
print hello

.sub _main
    hello = "Hello, Polly.\n"
    print hello
    end
.end
```

In the first line of this example, the .local directive defines a file global variable named hello. The _main routine uses the same variable, and would give you a parse error if it hadn't been defined. "Polly want a cracker?" is never assigned to the variable and printed.

Pure PASM compilation units can use the .emit and .eom directives instead of .sub and .end:

```
.emit
    print "Hello, Polly.\n"
    end
.eom
```

The .emit directive doesn't take a name.

The section coming up on "Subroutines" goes into much more detail about compilation units and their uses.

Scope and Namespaces

The .namespace directive creates a scoped namespace for variables. Variables from outside the namespace are visible in the inner scope unless that scope has a local variable with the same name:

```
.sub _scoped_hello
    .local PerlString hello
    hello = new PerlString
    hello = "Welcome, Python!\n"
    .namespace inner
    .local PerlString hello
    hello = new PerlString
    hello = "Hello, Perl 6.\n"
    print hello
    .endnamespace inner
    print hello
    end
.end
```

This example prints:

```
Hello, Perl 6.
Welcome, Python!
```

The first .local directive defines a named variable hello in the default outer namespace. The second .local defines a named variable in the inner namespace. Internally, it actually mangles the name of the variable as inner::hello. The first print is nested in the inner namespace, so it prints inner::hello, "Hello, Perl 6." The second print statement retrieves the hello variable of the outer namespace, so it prints "Welcome, Python!"

Constants are collected for the whole program so they can be efficiently folded. Identical string or number constants in different compilation units get a single entry in the constant table.

Flow Control

As in PASM, flow control in PIR is done entirely with conditional and unconditional branches. This may seem simplistic, but remember PIR is a thin overlay on the assembly language of a virtual processor. For the average assembly language, the jump is the fundamental unit of flow control.

Any PASM branch instruction is valid, but IMCC has some high-level constructs of its own. The most basic is the unconditional branch: goto.

```
.sub _main
    goto L1
    print "never printed"
L1:
    print "after branch\n"
    end
.end
```

The first print statement never runs because the goto always skips over it to the label L1.

The conditional branches combine if or unless with goto.

```
.sub _main
    $I0 = 42
    if $I0 goto L1
    print "never printed"
L1: print "after branch\n"
    end
.end
```

In this example, the goto branches to the label L1 only if the value stored in $I0 is true. The unless statement is quite similar, but branches when the tested value is false. An undefined value, 0, or an empty string are all false values. The if ... goto statement is translated directly to Parrot's if, and unless translates to Parrot's unless.

The comparison operators (<, <=, ==, !=, >, >=) combine with if ... goto. These branch when the comparison is true:

```
.sub _main
    $I0 = 42
    $I1 = 43
    if $I0 < $I1 goto L1
    print "never printed"
L1:
    print "after branch\n"
    end
.end
```

This example compares $I0 to $I1 and branches to the label L1 if $I0 is less than $I1. The if $I0 < $I1 goto L1 statement translates directly to the PASM lt branch operation.

The rest of the comparison operators are summarized at the end of this chapter.

PIR has no special loop constructs. A combination of conditional and unconditional branches handle iteration:

```
.sub _main
    $I0 = 1               # product
    $I1 = 5               # counter

REDO:                     # start of loop
    $I0 = $I0 * $I1
    dec $I1
    if $I1 > 0 goto REDO  # end of loop

    print $I0
    print "\n"
    end
.end
```

This example calculates the factorial 5!. Each time through the loop it multiplies $I0 by the current value of the counter $I1, decrements the counter, and then branches to the start of the loop. The loop ends when $I1 counts down to 0 and the if doesn't branch to REDO. This is a *do while*-style loop with the condition test at the end, so the code always runs the first time through.

For a *while*-style loop with the condition test at the start, use a conditional branch together with an unconditional branch:

```
.sub _main
    $I0 = 1        # product
    $I1 = 5        # counter
```

```
REDO:                          # start of loop
     if $I1 <= 0 goto LAST
     $I0 = $I0 * $I1
     dec $I1
     goto REDO
LAST:                          # end of loop

     print $I0
     print "\n"
     end
.end
```

This example tests the counter $I1 at the start of the loop. At the end of the loop, it unconditionally branches back to the start of the loop and tests the condition again. The loop ends when the counter $I1 reaches 0 and the if branches to the LAST label. If the counter isn't a positive number before the loop, the loop never executes.

Any high-level flow control construct can be built from conditional and unconditional branches.

Subroutines

A calculation like "the factorial of a number" may be used several times in a large program. Subroutines allow this kind of functionality to be abstracted into a unit. It's a benefit for code reuse and generally makes it easier to work with the code too. Even though PASM is just an assembly language running on a virtual processor, it has a number of features to support high-level subroutine calls. IMCC offers a smoother interface to those features.

Stack-Based Subroutine Calls

Unlike most high-level languages, PIR and PASM don't provide a single statement to call a subroutine, pass in the arguments, and return the result. This is a language designed to implement other languages, and every language does subroutine calls a little differently. What's needed is a set of building blocks and tools, not a prepackaged solution.

PIR has several directives and instructions relevant to subroutine calls. The most important is call, which simply branches to a subroutine label. On the side of the caller, .arg passes an argument to a subroutine, and .result retrieves a result. Within the subroutine, .param retrieves an argument passed to the subroutine, and .return returns a value to the caller:

```
.sub _main
    .local int counter
    counter = 5
```

```
        .arg counter        # pass an argument
        call _fact          # call the subroutine
        .local int product
        .result product     # retrieve the result
        print product
        print "\n"
        end
    .end

    .sub _fact
        saveall             # save caller's registers
        .param int N        # retrieve the parameter
        .local int prod
        prod = 1
    REDO:
        prod = prod * N
        dec N
        if N > 0 goto REDO
        .return prod        # return the result
        restoreall          # restore caller's registers
        ret                 # back to the caller
    .end
```

This example reimplements the factorial code from the previous section as
an independent subroutine. The subroutine _fact is a separate compilation
unit, assembled and processed after the _main function. IMCC resolves global symbols like the _fact label between different units.

The _main compilation unit sets up a local variable named counter and
passes it to the subroutine using the .arg directive. This is just the PASM
save instruction—it pushes the argument onto the user stack. It then calls
_fact with the call instruction. This is PASM's bsr. It branches to a sub-
routine label and pushes the current location onto the control stack so it
can return to it later.

The .result directive saves the value returned by the subroutine in the variable named product. This is just the PASM restore instruction—it pops a
return value off the user stack. The common case for return values is to use
an existing local variable, so .result doesn't create a new named variable.

The first statement in the _fact subroutine is saveall. This saves all the
registers off to the typed stacks, so they can be restored at the end of the
subroutine. This is a callee save—the subroutine takes responsibility for
preserving the environment of the caller. The advantage here is that IMCC
can ignore the subroutine's register usage when it allocates registers for the
_main routine—a call or bsr instruction has as much impact on register
allocation as a noop.

The next statement is .param, which pops a function parameter off the user stack as an integer. The .param directive also creates a new named local variable for the parameter. So the statement:

```
.param int N
```

is exactly the same as:

```
.local int N
restore N
```

which explicitly defines a local named integer variable and then calls the PASM restore to pop a value off the user stack. IMCC doesn't check the type, order, or number of the parameters to make sure they match what the the caller passes to the subroutine. You'll get no warning for a mismatch.

The next section is the same loop we had in the earlier example to calculate a factorial, but now it uses the parameter passed in to the subroutine as the counter. The .return statement at the end returns the final value of prod to the caller. This is just the PASM save instruction again—it pushes the value onto the user stack, so .result can retrieve it after the subroutine ends. restoreall restores the caller's register values, and ret pops the top item off the control stack—in this case, the location of the call to _fact—and goes back to it.

When you have more then one argument to pass to the subroutine, passing order is the reverse of retrieval order. You push the final argument onto the user stack first, because it'll be the last parameter popped off the stack on the other end. Multiple return values are also passed in reverse order for the same reason. Often the first parameter or result will be a count of values passed in, especially when the number of arguments can vary:

```
.arg y          # save args in reverse order
.arg x
call _foo       # (r, s) = _foo(x,y)
.result r
.result s       # restore results in order
```

The example above could have been written using simple labels instead of separate compilation units:

```
.sub _main
    $I1 = 5        # counter
    call fact      # same as bsr fact
    print $I0
    print "\n"
    $I1 = 6        # counter
    call fact
    print $I0
    print "\n"
    end
```

```
fact:
    $I0 = 1              # product
L1:
    $I0 = $I0 * $I1
    dec $I1
    if $I1 > 0 goto L1
    ret
.end
```

The unit of code from the fact label definition to ret is a reusable routine, but there are several problems with this simple approach. First, the caller has to know to pass the argument to fact in $I1 and to get the result from $I0. Second, neither the caller nor the function itself preserves any registers. This is fine for the example above, because very few registers are used. But if this same bit of code were buried deeply in a math routine package, you would have a high risk of clobbering the caller's register values.

Another disadvantage of this approach is that _main and fact share the same compilation unit, so they're parsed and processed as one piece of code. When IMCC does register allocation, it calculates the data flow graph (DFG) of all symbols,* looks at their usage, calculates the interference between all possible combinations of symbols, and then assigns a Parrot register to each symbol. This process is less efficient for large compilation units than it is for several small ones, so it's better to keep the code modular. The optimizer will decide whether register usage is light enough to merit combining two compilation units, or even inlining the entire function.

A Short Note on the Optimizer

The optimizer isn't powerful enough to inline small subroutines yet. But it already does other simpler optimizations. You may recall that the PASM opcode mul (multiply) has a two-argument version that uses the same register for the destination and the first operand. When IMCC comes across a PIR statement like $I0 = $I0 * $I1, it can optimize it to the two-argument mul $I0, $I1 instead of mul $I0, $I0, $I1. This kind of optimization is enabled by the -01 command-line option.

So you don't need to worry about finding the shortest PASM instruction, calculating constant terms, or avoiding branches to speed up your code. IMCC does it already.

---

* The operation to calculate the DFG has a cost of $O(2)$ or better. It depends on $n\_lines * n\_symbols$.

Parrot Calling Conventions

Parrot defines a set of calling conventions for all subroutines that are externally visible. Since these routines may be called as part of a library or module, it's important to have a consistent interface. In these calls, the caller is responsible for preserving its own registers, and arguments and return values are passed in a predefined set of Parrot registers.

IMCC's implementation of the Parrot calling conventions is still unfinished. The example here is mostly PASM, but the comments show the planned IMCC syntax:

```
.sub _main
    .local int count
    .local int product
    count = 5
    product = 1

    saveall
    I5 = count              # .nciarg count
    I6 = product            # .nciarg product

    .local Sub factsub
    factsub = new Sub

    $I0 = addr _fact
    factsub = $I0

    P0 = factsub            # .ncicall factsub  # fact(count, product)
    invoke

    save I5                 # .nciresult $I0
    restoreall
    restore $I0

    print $I0
    print "\n"
    end
.end


.sub _fact
loop:
    if I6 <= 1 goto fin
    I5 = I5 * I6
    dec I6
    branch loop
fin:
    ret
.end
```

The directives .nciarg, .ncicall, and .nciresult aren't implemented yet, but it's likely that they will be by the time you read this.

Let's take a closer look at the individual parts of this example. First, two locally named variables are defined and assigned values. All registers are preserved with the saveall instruction. The function call sequence begins with:

```
I5 = count      # .nciarg count
I6 = product    # .nciarg product
```

The arguments to _fact are assigned to consecutive registers, starting with I5. Next, a variable of class Sub is created. IMCC's = addr syntax gets the branch offset to a label, just like PASM's set_addr. The value assigned to the factsub variable sets the offset of the subroutine it will invoke. Since the subroutine is its own compilation unit, a fixup of the global label _fact is done just before emitting the actual code.

The invoke opcode does a function call with the function object in the parrot register P0—it pushes the offset of the next instruction onto the control stack and branches to the subroutine.

On returning from the subroutine, the return value is saved, registers get restored, and the result is printed.

PASM Subroutines

We mentioned earlier that pure PASM compilation units can use the .emit and .eom directives instead of .sub and .end. These can be useful for grouping PASM functions or function wrappers. The subroutine entry labels have to be global labels:

```
.emit
_substr:
    ...
    ret
_grep:
    ...
    ret
.eom
```

IMCC Command-Line Options

Since IMCC is both an assembler and a Parrot bytecode interpreter, it has options to control both behaviors. Some options may have changed by the time you read this, especially options related to debugging and optimization. The document *languages/imcc/docs/running.pod* should have the latest details.

General Usage

```
imcc [options] file [arguments]
```

The *file* is either an *.imc* or *.pasm* source file or a Parrot bytecode file. Parrot creates a `PerlArray` object to hold the command-line *arguments* and stores it in `P0` on program start.

Assembler Options

`-a,--pasm`

Assume PASM input on `stdin`. When IMCC runs a source file with a *.pasm* extension, it parses the file as pure PASM code. This switch turns on PASM parsing (instead of the default PIR parsing) when a source file is read from `stdin`.

`-c,--pbc`

Assume PBC file on `stdin`. When IMCC runs a bytecode file with a *.pbc* extension, it immediately executes the file. This option tells IMCC to immediately execute a bytecode file piped in on `stdin`.

`-d,--debug [hexbits]`

Turn on debugging output. The `-d` switch takes an optional argument, which is a hex value of debug bits. The individual bits are shown in Table 7-1. When *hexbits* isn't specified, the default debugging level is 0001. If the *hexbits* is separated from the `-d` switch by whitespace, it has to start with a number.

Table 7-1. Debug bits

Description	Debug bit
DEBUG_PARROT	0001
DEBUG_LEXER	0002
DEBUG_PARSER	0004
DEBUG_IMC	0008
DEBUG_CFG	0010
DEBUG_OPT1	0020
DEBUG_OPT2	0040
DEBUG_PBC	1000
DEBUG_PBC_CONST	2000
DEBUG_PBC_FIXUP	4000

To produce a huge output on `stderr`, turn on all the debugging bits:

```
$ imcc -d 0ffff ...
```

-h,--help
> Print a short summary of options to stdout and exit.

-o *outputfile*
> Act like an assembler. With this switch IMCC won't run code unless it's combined with the -r switch. If the name of *outputfile* ends with a *.pbc* extension, IMCC writes a Parrot bytecode file. If *outputfile* ends with a *.pasm* extension, IMCC writes a PASM source file, even if the input file was also PASM. This can be handy to check various optimizations when you run IMCC with the -Op switch.

-r,--run-pbc
> Immediately execute bytecode. This is the default unless -o is present. The combination of -r -o output.pbc writes a bytecode file and executes the program.

-v,--verbose
> One -v switch (imcc -v) shows which files are worked on and prints a summary of register usage and optimization statistics. Two -v switches (imcc -v -v) also prints a line for each individual processing step.

-y,--yydebug
> Turn on yydebug for *yacc/bison*.

-V,--version
> Print the program version to stdout and exit.

-0*x*
> Turn on optimizations. The flags currently implemented are shown in Table 7-2.

Table 7-2. Optimizations

Flag	Meaning
-O0	No optimization (default).
-O1	Optimizations without life info (e.g., branches and constants).
-O2	Optimizations with life info.
-Op	Rearrange PASM registers with the most-used first.

Bytecode Interpreter Options

The interpreter options are mainly for selecting which runtime core to use for interpreting bytecode. The current default is the *computed goto core* if it's available. Otherwise the *fast core* is used.

-b Activate bounds checking. This also runs with the *slow core* as a side effect.

-g Deactivate the *computed goto core* (CGoto) and run with the *fast core*.

-j Run with the *JIT core* if available.

-p Activate profiling. This prints a summary of opcode usage and execution times after the program stops. It also runs within the *slow core*.

-P Run with the *CGoto-Prederefed* core if it's available. Otherwise run with the *Prederefed core*.

-S Run with the *Switched core*.

-t Trace execution. This also turns on the *slow core*.

-. Wait for a keypress before running.

IMCC Quick Reference

This is a summary of PIR directives and instructions. Any PASM opcode is valid in PIR code, so you should also look at "Writing Tests" in Chapter 6. For more details and the latest changes, see *languages/imcc/docs/syntax.pod* or dive into the source code in *languages/imcc/imcc.l* and *languages/imcc/imcc.y*.

Directives

.arg

`.arg VAL`

Push a value onto the user stack.

.const

`.const TYPE NAME = VALUE`

Define a named constant.

.constant

`.constant NAME VALUE`

Define a named macro that expands to a given value. Macros are called as directives, so `.NAME` (PASM code only).

.emit

`.emit`

Define a compilation unit of PASM code. Always paired with `.eom`.

.end

`.end`

End a compilation unit. Always paired with `.sub`.

.endm

`.endm`

End a macro definition. Always paired with `.macro`.

.endnamespace

`.endnamespace` *NAME*

End a namespace. Always paired with `.namespace`.

.eom

`.eom`

End a compilation unit of PASM code. Always paired with `.emit`.

.include

`.include " ` *FILENAME* ` "`

Include the contents of an external file by inserting it in place.

.local

`.local` *TYPE NAME*

Define a local named variable.

.macro

`.macro NAME (PARAMS)`

Define a named macro with a list of parameters. The macro is called as `.NAME` (*arg1,arg2,...*). Always paired with `.endm`. (PASM code only.)

.namespace

`.namespace NAME`

Define a namespace. Always paired with `.endnamespace`.

.param

`.param DEST`
`.param TYPE NAME`

Pop a value off the user stack into a register or typed identifier.

.result

`.result DEST`

Pop a value off the user stack.

.return

`.return VAL`

Return a value to the calling subroutine by pushing it onto the user stack.

.sub

`.sub NAME`

Define a compilation unit. Always paired with `.end`. Names begin with "_" by convention.

.sym

`.sym TYPE NAME`

Same as `.local`.

Instructions

=

`DEST = VAL`

Assign a value to a particular register, temporary register, or named variable.

+

`DEST = VAL + VAL`

Add two numbers or PMCs.

-

`DEST = VAL1 - VAL2`
`DEST = - VAL`

Subtract *VAL1* from *VAL2*. The unary "-" negates a number.

---

*

`DEST = VAL * VAL`

Multiply two numbers or PMCs.

/

`DEST = VAL1 / VAL2`

Divide *VAL1* by *VAL2*.

**

`DEST = VAL1 ** VAL2`

Raise *VAL1* to the power of *VAL2*.

%

`DEST = VAL1 % VAL2`

Divide *VAL1* by *VAL2* and return the (mod) remainder.

.

`DEST = VAL . VAL`

Concatenate two strings.

<

`if VAL1 < VAL2 goto LABEL`

Conditionally branch to a label if VAL1 is less than VAL2.

<=

`if VAL1 <= VAL2 goto LABEL`

Conditionally branch to a label if VAL1 is less than or equal to VAL2.

>

`if VAL1 > VAL2 goto LABEL`

Conditionally branch to a label if VAL1 is greater than VAL2.

>=

`if VAL1 >= VAL2 goto LABEL`

Conditionally branch to a label if VAL1 is greater than or equal to VAL2.

==

`if VAL1 == VAL2 goto LABEL`

Conditionally branch to a label if VAL1 is equal to VAL2.

!=

`if VAL1 != VAL2 goto LABEL`

Conditionally branch to a label if VAL1 is not equal to VAL2.

&&

DEST = VAL1 && *VAL2*

Logical AND. Return *VAL1* if it's false, *VAL2* if *VAL1* is true.

||

DEST = VAL1 || *VAL2*

Logical OR. Return *VAL1* if it's true, *VAL2* if *VAL1* is false.

~~

DEST = VAL1 ~~ *VAL2*

Logical XOR. Return *VAL1* if it's true and *VAL2* is false. Return *VAL2* if *VAL2* is true and *VAL1* is false. Otherwise, return false.

!

DEST = ! *VAL*

Logical NOT. Return a true value if *VAL* is false.

&

DEST = VAL & *VAL*

Bitwise AND on two values.

|

DEST = VAL | *VAL*

Bitwise OR on two values.

~

DEST = VAL ~ *VAL*
DEST = ~ *VAL*

Bitwise XOR on two values. The unary form is a bitwise NOT on a value.

<<

```
DEST = VAL1 << VAL2
```

Bitwise shift *VAL1* left by *VAL2* number of bits.

>>

```
DEST = VAL1 >> VAL2
```

Bitwise shift *VAL1* right by *VAL2* number of bits.

>>>

```
DEST = VAL1 >>> VAL2
```

Logically shift *VAL1* right by *VAL2* number of bits.

[ ]

```
DEST = PMC [ KEY ]
PMC [ KEY ] = VAL
```

Indexed access to a PMC and indexed assignment to a PMC.

```
DEST = STRING [ OFFSET ]
STRING [ OFFSET ]  = VAL
```

Access a one-character substring on a string, starting at a particular offset, or assign to that substring.

addr

```
DEST = addr LABEL
```

Return the address of a label.

call

```
call NAME
```

Call the named subroutine (a .sub label).

clone

```
DEST = clone VAL
```

Create a clone of a variable.

defined

`DEST = defined VAL`

Test a value or keyed value for definedness.

global

`DEST = global NAME`
`global NAME = VAL`

Access a global for read or write.

goto

`goto NAME`

Jump to the named identifier (label or subroutine name).

if

`if EXPR goto NAME`

If the value or expression evaluates as true, jump to the named identifier.

new

`DEST = new TYPE`

Create a new PMC of type TYPE.

unless

`unless VAL goto NAME`

Unless the value evaluates as true, jump to the named identifier.

Index

Symbols

= = instruction (IMCC), 183
[ ] instruction (IMCC), 185
& ("all" junction) operator, 38
[...] (anonymous arrayref
      constructor), 29
| ("any" junction) operator, 38
@_ array, 53
?& (boolean AND) operator, 35
?| (boolean OR) operator, 35
?^ (boolean XOR) operator, 35
% format strings for sprintf opcode, 107
! instruction (IMCC), 184
!= instruction (IMCC), 183
% instruction (IMCC), 182
& instruction (IMCC), 184
&& instruction (IMCC), 184
* instruction (IMCC), 182
** instruction (IMCC), 182
+ instruction (IMCC), 182
- instruction (IMCC), 182
. instruction (IMCC), 183
/ instruction (IMCC), 182
< instruction (IMCC), 183
<< instruction (IMCC), 185
<= instruction (IMCC), 183
= instruction (IMCC), 182
> instruction (IMCC), 183
>= instruction (IMCC), 183
>> instruction (IMCC), 185
>>> instruction (IMCC), 185
| instruction (IMCC), 184

|| instruction (IMCC), 184
// null pattern, 67
^ ("one" junction) operator, 38
! operator, 36
% operator, 33
%= operator, 33
* operator, 33, 45
** operator, 33
**= operator, 33
*= operator, 33
+ operator, 33, 37
+& operator, 37
+&= operator, 37
+= operator, 33
+^ operator, 37
+^= operator, 37
+| operator, 37
+|= operator, 37
- operator, 33
-= operator, 33
/ operator, 33
// operator, 35
/= operator, 33
:= operator, 33
<< operator, 37
<<= operator, 37
= operator, 32
>> operator, 37
? operator, 36
??:: operator, 37
|| (OR) operator, 35
$ sigil, variables with, 28
% sigil, variables with, 28, 30

We'd like to hear your suggestions for improving our indexes. Send email to *index@oreilly.com*.

filehandle, 26
find_global opcode, 142
find_lex opcode, 122, 123, 142
find_method opcode, 142
find_type opcode, 142
flattening list context, 36
flow control
    construct, 92
    in PIR, 169–171
for loop, 49
formal parameters, 53
freedom, principle of, 22

G

garbage collection
    Parrot, 90
        PMC and, 90
gcd opcode, 102, 143
gc_debug opcode, 143
ge opcode, 116, 143
general purpose stack, 118
get_bool vtable method, 116
getfile opcode, 142
getline opcode, 142
getpackage opcode, 143
getprop opcode, 114, 143
global instruction (IMCC), 186
goto command (IMCC), 169, 186
grammars and rules, 61–69
greater-than operator (>, gt), 34
greater-than-or-equal operator
        (>=, ge), 34
gt opcode, 116, 143

H

Hansen, Ask Björn, 8
hashes, 26
    matching, 43
hashlist context, 30, 36
hashrefs, 28
hav opcode, 143
high-speed intstack, 119
hypothetical variables, 68

I

if opcode, 116, 144
if statement, 46
    (IMCC), 186
.imc files, 158

IMCC (Intermediate Code
        Compiler), 158–186
    assembler options, 177
    bytecode interpreter options, 178
    command-line options, 176–179
    comments, 160
    compiling, 158
    debugging bits, 177
    directives to, 168
    documentation, 159
    labels, 166
    named constants, 164
    named variables, 163
    namespaces, 168
    optimizations, 178
    overview, 159
    Parrot classes and, 163
    quick reference, 179–186
    register allocation, 174
    register spilling, 165
    scope, 168
    statements, 160
    subroutines, 171–176
        Parrot calling conventions, 175
    temporary registers, 161
inc opcode, 144
.include directive, 180
index opcode, 108, 144
inequality operator (!=, ne), 34
inheritance, 60
intdepth opcode, 119, 144
integer bitwise operators, 37
integer context, 36
integer stack, 119
Intermediate Code Compiler (see IMCC)
interpinfo opcode, 144
interpreter, Parrot, 76–81
    registers, 76
    stacks, 77
    strings, 78
    variables, 79
intrestore opcode, 119, 145
intsave opcode, 119, 145
invoke opcode, 145
    coroutines and, 131
I/O
    failure, 109
    Parrot's, 82
iteration, 48–50
    in PASM, 117

J

jsr opcode, 124, 145
jump opcode, 145
junctions, 39
    matching, 44
    operators, 38
junctive operations in scalar context, 38

K

KEEP property block, 53
keyed access to PMCs, 112

L

labels in IMCC, 166
language
    borrowing, 22
    culture and, 21
    design, 9
    linguistic and cognitive
        considerations of Perl
        6, 16–22
last keyword, 50
lazy list context, 35, 36
Lazzaro, Michael, 7
lcm opcode, 102, 145
le opcode, 116, 145
length opcode, 104, 146
less-than operator (<, lt), 34
less-than-or-equal operator (<=, le), 34
let command, 51
lexical subroutines, 56
lexically scoped subroutines, 56
lexing, 72
list context, 29, 36
    lazy, 35
    non-flattening, 35
lists, matching, 41
ln opcode, 146
loadlib opcode, 128, 146
.local directive, 180
log10 opcode, 146
log2 opcode, 146
logical opcodes, 110
logical operators, 34
lookback opcode, 118, 146

loops, 49
    breaking out of, 50
    PASM, 117
    PIR, 170
lsr opcode, 146
lt opcode, 116, 147
lvalues, using * on, 45

M

.macro directive, 181
mailing list, Perl 6, 5
_main compilation unit, 172
metacharacters, 62
metasymbols, 62
methods, 59
mixed class-type support in Parrot, 89
mod opcode, 102, 147
modifiers, 64
modulus operator (%), 33
mul opcode, 102, 147
multimethod, 56
    dispatching, 91
multiplication operator (*), 33
my keyword, 51

N

named constants in IMCC, 164
named variables (IMCC), 163
    Parrot classes and, 164
.namespace directive, 181
namespaces in IMCC, 168
NCI (Native Call Interface), 128
    function signatures, 128
.nciarg directive, 176
.ncicall directive, 176
.nciresult directive, 176
ne opcode, 116, 147
neg opcode, 147
nested scopes, 123
new instruction (IMCC), 186
new method, 58
new opcode, 147
newinterp opcode, 148
new_pad opcode, 122, 148
next keyword, 50
non-fatal signals, 85

non-flattening list context, 35, 36
noop opcode, 148
not opcode, 111, 148
null pattern //, 67
numeric context, 36

O

Object class, 58
object context, 36
objects, 58–61
    calling in different register, 128
    creating new, 58
    matching, 44
    Parrot, 87–89
opaque classes, 88
opcode, 80
open opcode, 109, 148
operators, 32–46
optimizations (IMCC), 178
optimizer, 73, 174
optimizing code for dynamic
        languages, 74
or opcode, 111, 148
or operator, 34
ord opcode, 106, 149
our keyword, 51

P

p6i (Perl 6 internals mailing list), 5
.param directive, 171, 173, 181
parameters
    formal, 53
    passing, 55
Parrot, 6
    architecture, 71–75
    base class, 89
    bug tracking, 15
    bytecode, 81
    bytecode, creating, 158
    bytecode loader, 75
    classes
        clone and, 164
        IMCC and, 163
        inheritance, 99
    compiler module, 72, 73
    core design principles, 70
    dead object detection system, 90
    development, 11–15
    getting involved, 12–15

internals, 70–93
interpreter (see interpreter, Parrot)
loadable opcode library system, 75
native data type (see PMCs)
optimizer module, 73
parser module, 72
patch submission, 13–15
stacks and registers (see registers;
        stacks)
subroutine calling conventions, 126
Parrot assembly (see PASM)
Parrot Intermediate Language (see PIR)
Parrot Magic Cookies (see PMCs)
ParrotIO object, 109
Parrot::Test module, 133
parser, Parrot, 72
parsing text, 69
.pasm files, 95, 159
PASM (Parrot assembly
        language), 94–157
    bitwise operations, 110
    comments, 96
    compiling, 95
    conditional branches, 116
    constants, 96
    flow control, 115–117
    global variables, 121
    I/O operations, 109
    iteration, 117
    label definitions, 96
    lexical variables, 122–124
    logical operations, 110
    loops, 117
    math operations, 101–102
        binary, 102
        floating-point, 102
    opcodes, quick references, 134–157
    overview, 95–111
    registers, 96–100, 161
        assignment, 97
        difference between temporary
            register variables and, 161
    source code, 94
    string operations, 103–109
        chopping strings, 105
        concatenation, 103
        converting strings, 106
        copying, 106
        formatting strings, 106–108
        length, 104

About the Authors

Allison Randal is the assistant project manager of the Perl 6 core development team. She has been working closely with Damian Conway and Larry Wall on Perl 6 and has cowritten the "synopses" of Perl 6. She is dedicated to the success of the project and is one of the very first to learn about anything new that's proposed for Perl 6.

Dan Sugalski is the chief architect for Parrot, the interpreter engine for Perl 6. He's been a Perl 5 core developer for years, writing more than a dozen modules in the process. He's been a contributor to *The Perl Journal* and *The Perl Review*, as well as the O'Reilly Network.

Leopold Tötsch hails from Austria, where he first started working with computers in 1976. He is an independent software developer who has been exploring and developing open source software since 1991. He's a frequent contributor to isdnlog (an open source project for monitoring ISDN lines and optimizing telephone costs) and spends the majority of his free time working on Parrot, the language-independent interpreter developed as part of the Perl 6 design strategy.

Colophon

Our look is the result of reader comments, our own experimentation, and feedback from distribution channels. Distinctive covers complement our distinctive approach to technical topics, breathing personality and life into potentially dry subjects.

The animal on the cover of *Perl 6 Essentials* is an aoudad (*ammotragus lervia*). Commonly known as Barbary sheep, aoudads originated in the arid mountainous regions of northern Africa and have stout, sturdy bodies, standing 75–100 centimeters at the shoulder and weighing from 30–145 kilograms. The aoudad has a bristly reddish-brown coat and is distinguished by a heavy, fringed mane covering its chest and legs. Both males and females have thick, triangular-shaped horns that curve back in a semicircle. A male aoudad's horns can grow up to 85 centimeters.

Aoudads are herbivores and are most active at dawn and dusk, avoiding the desert heat of midday. They will drink water if it is available, but can obtain sufficient moisture from dew and vegetation. Aoudads are incredible jumpers, able to clear 6 feet from a standstill. So well suited are they to their surroundings that newborns have the ability to navigate rocky slopes within just hours after birth.

Despite being endangered in their native environment, aoudads are flourishing in the United States. Introduced to western Texas and southern New Mexico in the 1940s, aoudads are now so populous that it is feared that their presence may threaten the native desert bighorn sheep. Aoudads are considered native game in the desert mountains of their adopted home, where the rugged landscape is dotted with ranches catering to recreational hunters.

Emily Quill was the production editor, and Sarah Jane Shangraw was the copyeditor for *Perl 6 Essentials*. Phil Dangler and Mary Anne Weeks Mayo provided quality control. Jamie Peppard provided production assistance. Julie Hawks wrote the index.

Ellie Volckhausen designed the cover of this book, based on a series design by Edie Freedman. The cover image is a 19th-century engraving from *Animate Creations, Volume II*. Emma Colby produced the cover layout with QuarkXPress 4.1 using Adobe's ITC Garamond font.

David Futato designed the interior layout. This book was converted by Andrew Savikas to FrameMaker 5.5.6 with a format conversion tool created by Erik Ray, Jason McIntosh, Neil Walls, and Mike Sierra that uses Perl and XML technologies. The text font is Linotype Birka; the heading font is Adobe Myriad Condensed; and the code font is LucasFont's TheSans Mono Condensed. The illustrations that appear in the book were produced by Robert Romano and Jessamyn Read using Macromedia FreeHand 9 and Adobe Photoshop 6. This colophon was written by Emily Quill.